We Worship As We Live
A Devotional Journey Through the Years

We Worship As We Live
A Devotional Journey Through the Years

by Pastor Carl H. Lee

Concordia College
MOORHEAD, MINNESOTA

*To all the students who, through my 34-year ministry here,
worshiped as they lived.*

*To my family who, for 34 years,
enabled and encouraged this ministry of worship.*

WE WORSHIP AS WE LIVE
A Devotional Journey Through the Years

Copyright © 1996 Concordia College. All rights reserved. Except for brief quotations in critical articles or reviews, no part of this book may be reproduced or transmitted in any form or by any means, electronic or mechanical, including photocopying, recording or by any information storage or retrieval system, without permission in writing from the publisher:

> Concordia College
> 901 South Eighth Street
> Moorhead, MN 56562

Photographs and other illustrative matters are copyrighted by the individual photographer or artist.

Unless otherwise noted, Scripture quotations are from the New Revised Standard Version Bible, copyright 1989 Division of Christian Education of the National Council of the Churches of Christ in the United States of America. Used by permission.

Cover and interior design: Hetland Ltd., Fargo, North Dakota
Separations and printing: Kaye's Printing, Fargo, North Dakota

---

Library of Congress Cataloging-in-Publication Data

Lee, Carl H., 1930-
    We worship as we live: a devotional journey through the years / Carl H. Lee.
      88 p.
      ISBN 0-9630111-1-1
      1. Lee, Carl H. 2. Concordia College (Moorhead, Minn.). 3. Lutheran Church — Sermons.
    4. Sermons, American. 5. Church work with students — Lutheran Church. 6. Universities and colleges.
I. Concordia College (Moorhead, Minn.) II. Title
BV 4310 .L44 1996
252.04135

Manufactured in the U.S.A.

Contents

Introduction by Dr. Paul J. Dovre/**ii**

Author's Preface/**iii**

AUGUST — Preludes
Hosting/**1** Becoming/**2** Praying/**4** Serving/**5** Inviting/**6** Beginning/**7**

SEPTEMBER — Invitations
Remember . . . You Count!/**8** This New Day/**9** An Evening Psalm/**10**
Run with Perseverance/**11** A Crystal Gaze/**13** Ties Never End/**14**
Always a Parent/**15** A 'Whobody' Visit/**16** Risk Taking a Chance/**17**

OCTOBER — Responses
Come! Celebrate the Spirit!/**18** A Truly Happy Cobber/**19**
That Special Championship Season/**20** We Dedicate This Building/**21**
A Psalm of Relaxation/**22** Kyrie! Heal!/**23** Unexpected Interruptions/**24**

NOVEMBER — Kyries
On Taking a Break/**26** Praying Goodbyes/**27** Thank You/**28** Have Mercy/**29**
Slow Down/**30** Simple Gifts/**31**

DECEMBER — Glorias
Don't Just Do Something! Stand There!/**32** Things That Make for Christmas Peace/**34**
Come Home with Me for Christmas/**35** Through the Eyes of a Child/**37**

JANUARY — Introits
Magi and Graduates . . . Follow a Star/**38** The Magic Slate/**39**
Blessed Are You/**40** Magi Journey Eastward/**41**
In Loving Memory/**43** Morning and Evening/**44** Come, Lord Jesus/**45**

FEBRUARY — Lessons
Are You Listening?/**46** I Wonder About . . ./**47**
Be My Valentine/**49** Mountaintops and Valleys/**50**
Living Bible Verses/**52** Good Guilt/**53**

MARCH — Confessions
Encouraging Words/**54** Special Crosses/**55** Mommy! Daddy!/**56**
Mary! Martha!/**58** Extravagant Love/**59**

APRIL — Offertories
An Aloha Easter Experience/**61** A Prayer for Spring/**62**
Going the Extra Mile/**63** You Have Done Marvelously/**64**
Look at Us Now/**66** Be Gracious . . . Not Grumpy/**67**

MAY — Benedictions
Exodus Thank-Yous/**68** A Baccalaureate Surrounding/**69**
A Baccalaureate Blessing/**70** A Senior's Send-off/**71**
To the Graduates/**72** Go with God/**74**

SUMMER — Postludes
I Promise You/**76** What a Day!/**77** God's Glorious Fireworks/**79**
Ebbing and Flowing/**81** On Eagle's Wings/**82** In Retrospect/**85**

Special Thanks/**86**

Image Notes and Credits/**87**

About the Author/**Back Cover**

Introduction
by Dr. Paul J. Dovre
Concordia College President

In his 34-year ministry at Concordia, the Rev. Carl Lee ministered to more Cobbers than anyone else in the history of the college. He ministered to students from the roaring '60s, the somnambulant '70s, the anxious '80s and the naughty '90s. He ministered to Baby Boomers and Generation Xers. He survived the therapy of "I'm OK, you're OK," situational ethics, confrontational politics, feel-good religion and Twelve Steps to almost anything. He transcended every kind of music imaginable, including Christian rock, folk rock and rock rock — but he was saved from Christian rap!

All of this is not to say that Carl did not change or roll with the tide. As one of his mentors once said, a racehorse must know when to change speeds, and Carl understood that. But with respect to the basics, Carl was consistent, solid and dependable in a ministry evoked by these words from the Apostle Paul to the Ephesians:

> *I pray that, according to the riches of his glory, he may grant that you may be strengthened in your inner being with power through his Spirit, and that Christ may dwell in your hearts through faith, as you are being rooted and grounded in love.* — Ephesians 3:16-17

How did Carl Lee share such unique gifts? When I think of his outstanding ministry, it strikes me that Carl has been firmly "rooted and grounded" in people — people with unique names, individual needs, distinctive souls and distinguished gifts.

Second, Carl is "rooted and grounded" in community. He carried forward in his ministry some of the best qualities of Norwegian Lutheran piety: the piety of warm spirit, of hospitality, of experiential faith; the piety of coffee-and-cookies ministry; the piety of small talk, sports talk, political talk, weather talk — talk that binds and heals people, talk that builds community.

Finally, basic to all his ministry, Carl has been "rooted and grounded" in the gospel. Carl preached for us the gospel of "yes," the gospel of unconditional and overflowing acceptance, the gospel of affirmation, the gospel of calling — always rooted and grounded in love. And in all respects, he "worshiped as he lived." *Soli Deo Gloria.*

Preface
by Carl H. Lee

It was a familiar opening call to worship here.
It greeted so many of you when you began your freshman year.
It sent so many of you on your way when you graduated.
It was there through the rhythms and routines of your Concordia life.
It connected worship and life.
It is the title I have chosen for this book:

We Worship As We Live

Life during the school year parallels a worship in many ways:

Each has a predictable order and progression. From August's *Preludes* to May's *Benedictions,* the year mirrors the order of worship.

Each unfolds to reveal our own unique part in it. We truly do worship as we live!

This book chronicles the devotional journey that we have taken together through the years — and extends a personal invitation to continue along that path into each new day. Now and always, may *we worship as we live.*

Hosting

They are coming!
Almost a thousand strong! This year's freshman class!
Journeying with hope and dream to a new home at Concordia.

From the mountains of Montana, eastward across the plains of the Dakotas.
From the lakes of Minnesota and the urban sprawl of the Twin Cities.
From country and town, city and farm.
From earth's wide bounds, from ocean's farthest coast.
Future Cobbers . . . a countless host.

And here we are, the chosen and called ones, RAs and Communicators.
We are preparing to welcome them, the stranger, to Cord place — our home.
We are preparing to be hosts entertaining guests.
We are preparing how to practice hospitality so they can feel at home.
We are promising to surround them with love and hope.
We are promising to make these strangers our friends.

Here we are, passionate in learning how to be hospitable hosts.
Here we are, excited to provide friendship for our guests.
Here we are, joining hearts and dreams and hopes in harmony, *Concordially*.

We remember our freshman journey.
We remember what it was like to be a stranger in need of hospitality.
We remember what it was like to be a guest, needing hosting to be at home.
We remember what it was like to be surrounded, ourselves.
We remember how RA and Communicator hosted us with Concordia hospitality.

It is an incredible gift we RAs and Communicators have been given.
It is an incredible opportunity we have to be hosts offering hospitality.
It is an incredible ministry of caring to which our Lord is calling us.
We are ready to take on that ministry.

Let the freshmen come! Let our hosting begin!
Let strangers become friends! Let guests be made to feel at home!

Let our Lord respond to our hosting:

> ***I was a stranger and you welcomed me . . . just as you did it to one of the least of these who are members of my family, you did it to me.***
> — Matthew 25:35,40

Let future Cobbers begin their life here "on firm foundation grounded, with love and hope surrounded."

Becoming

How do freshmen anybodies become Concordia "*whobodies?*"

    First of all they need to come to Concordia.
    Then they get a roommate.
    Then they get a yellow beanie.
    Then they get into clubs . . .

        . . . where they get to know each other's names
    and share things about themselves
    and listen to each other
    and talk about what it means to live under the "C."

    Then they practice saying "Hi." and "How are you?" a lot.
    Then they really take time to listen and not rush off.
    Then they do all kinds of things together in their clubs.
    Then they do a really exciting "hands-for-change" thing.
    That makes them feel like they are really becoming "*whobodies!*"

    Sometimes somebody gets unexpected bad news about a mom or dad or family member or friend. Then everybody stops everything they're doing to remember that somebody in prayer. They'll call and offer to be there with, and for, that somebody in need. In that kind of reaching out and caring, people become very special "*whobodies.*"
    "*Whobodies*" become aware that when they are away from home, parents and families become more important "whobodies" to them. "Whobodies" call home and tell mom and dad and brothers and sisters that they miss them, and love them, and worry about them, and pray for them . . . even while they are enjoying being away from home here at Cord.

    Will you become a "*whobody*" this year?
    Will you be a "*whobody*" for somebody who may feel like a nobody or an anybody?
    Will you let others be "*whobodies*" for you?
    Will you let Jesus be a special "*whobody!*" for you . . .

        . . . always there for you and with you,
    caring for you and keeping you,
    loving you and helping you?

    Will you let Jesus be that special "*whobody*" who is here to cheer you on in this place of maroon and gold while he watches your life unfold?
    Remember who you are becoming: a special "*whobody*" living in Concordia's fields of dreams.

Praying

You are excited and you are scared.
You are glad and you are sad.
You are leaving your freshman child at Concordia.

You don't want to say goodbye yet.
You hang on to those reassuring words from the parents meeting:

> Pray your goodbyes before you say your goodbyes.
> Prayer is the greatest gift you can give your child now.
> Pray for them, and they'll pray for you.

> You are as close to your child as your prayers.
> Prayer spans the distances and keeps you connected.
> Prayer reassures your children that they'll never walk alone.

You say your goodbyes with aching love.
They say their goodbyes with eager anticipation.
You drive home praying your goodbyes.
They are already saying their hellos.

Goodbye for now! God be with you!
Hello again! I'm thinking of you and praying for you! *Amen.*

Serving

May your face, Lord, shine upon us and be gracious to us as we begin this new academic year.

> May you, Lord, take our lives and our gifts, our abilities and our commitment:
>
>> . . . to teach and lead
>> . . . to minister and serve
>> . . . to join hearts and minds Concordially, in harmony.
>
> May you, Lord, take our lights and let them be beams from you, the one true light.
>
> May you, Lord, take our many branches and let them be branches from you, the one tree.
>
> May you, Lord, take our many ways to serve, and let them be servant ways from you, the one true servant.
>
> May you, Lord, take our many members and let them be joined into one body, so that we are all one in you.
>
> May you, Lord, make our work this year another way of praying and another way of saying *"Soli Deo Gloria!"*
>
> May you, Lord, be our guest, and let this year to us be blessed. *Amen.*

Inviting

>Wednesday night . . . Communion night!
>Story and song . . . quiet time and listening time!
>Bread and wine . . . refreshment time and story time!

Tonight's story is "Suppertime — Come for Supper," adapted from an LCA publication *The Mood and Meaning of the Lord's Supper*. Relax, sit back and listen:

In the evening throughout the world the call is "Suppertime! Come for supper!"

Families and friends gather and join together for a meal and Communion . . . because there is more than just food to be shared.

Sitting around a room or table, or sharing a bench or dirt floor, families have companionship and conversation. The day's events are reviewed together. Tomorrow's possibilities are explored together. The family's needs are faced together.

>Healing and caring, love and hope
>Food and shelter, belonging and safety . . . are found together.

>Meanings and intentions, hopes and dreams
>Joys and sorrows, troubles and triumph . . . are shared together.

>Communion is experienced.

So it was one evening years ago, when at the invitation of their Lord, 12 people came to the intimate warmth of a special supper. They were more than friends. They were a family of companions and disciples.

In the midst of tensions and differences and anxiety and uncertainty, they were reconciled and renewed as they shared their Lord's supper.

So it is in this Communion tonight that we have come from all over the world, from coast to coast, from city and farm, at the invitation of this same Lord who invites us to the warmth of his supper and hosts us as his special guests.

We come as strangers who are welcomed as friends. We come as friends who welcome strangers to become new friends. We come as members of our new Cord family to be blessed as we share his supper.

>Feel burdens being lifted . . . belonging happening!
>Feel Christ's blessing . . . experience Christ's presence!
>Share Christ's peace . . . feel Christ's healing!

Jesus is present. Jesus is bringing us together into a new family. Our gracious host, Jesus himself, is calling us to his table for the family meal:

"Suppertime! I've prepared it especially for you! Come for supper!"

Beginning

O God, I begin my college career and a new academic year focused on and centered in *you*.

You! Only *you!* Always *you!*

When I wander, *you!*
When I ponder, *you!*
Only *you!* Always *you! You!*

When I am gladdened, *you!*
When I am saddened, *you!*
Only *you!* Always *you! You!*

In every trend, *you!*
At every end, *you!*
Only *you!* Always *you! You!*

When I need someone to guide me, *you!*
When I need someone beside me, *you!*
Only *you!* Always *you! You!*

When I struggle and I cry, *you!*
When I spread my wings and fly, *you!*
Only *you!* Always *you! You!*

O God, be present with me as I begin this school year.
Be beside me, in front of me, behind me, under me and over me.

You! Only *you!* Always *you!*
Thank *you! Amen.*

Remember . . . You Count!

Are not two sparrows sold for a penny?
Yet not one of them will fall to the ground apart from your Father.
So do not be afraid; you are of more value than many sparrows.
— Matthew 10:29, 31

If you have been feeling little since you came to Concordia . . . and if you have been wondering if God remembers you or cares about you . . . think of how a sparrow must feel. Have you ever heard someone say: "You know what? I saw the most beautiful sparrow today! And could that sparrow ever sing!"

Sparrows, for the most part, are ignored because there are so many of them. Because they all seem to look alike and sound the same, it's easy to tune them out. It's when a robin belts out a beautiful medley of song or a loon calls hauntingly that we stop to listen and take notice of their presence and gifts.

Yet God's promise today after the first few days of classes is that you are not tuned out or ignored. You are not so little and so numerous that you go unnoticed. God's promise to you is that you are remembered and watched over, you have worth and are loved. "Not a single one of you is forgotten by God. So do not be afraid. You are worth much more than many sparrows."

What a marvelous promise to claim and hold onto in your journey into and through this year: "You count too! You have worth! You are special! You are remembered!"

Do not fear. I have called you by name. You are precious in my sight . . .
and I love you. Do not fear, for I am with you.
— Isaiah 43:1,4,5

Remember that promise when you feel little and unnoticed. Remind yourself of that promise when you feel you are just one insignificant student among so many others who you think are smarter, more talented, more gifted and popular than you. Remember that promise when you feel yourself withdrawing and doubting yourself. Remind yourself of that promise when you feel alone and unappreciated.

Remember God's promise to you: "You count too! You really do! You have worth, you really do! You have gifts, you really do! You can make a difference, you really can! You have power, you really do! You can make it, you really can!"

Impossible? Not at all! Possible, yes! I'm possible. I really am!

That's what God promises: "For God all things are possible." — Mark 10:27 "All things can be done for the one who believes." — Mark 9:23 "I can do all things because Christ gives me the strength to do them." — Philippians 4:13 That's God's promise to you. Remember that!

Remember that promise when you get tired and anxious. Remind yourself of that promise when you go through tough times. Remember that promise when studying and practicing get you down. Remind yourself of that promise when you're doing well. God knows about you. God cares about you. God remembers you. God loves you just the way you are. You count too! Remember that!

This New Day

Before I awakened this morning, you were there with me, Lord, and even as I opened my eyes, you greeted me with the gift of this new day.

So another day begins, Lord, another journey from dawn to dusk in my life here. Here comes this new day with all its possibilities and opportunities.

It excites me and I welcome it as the day you made for me. I'll spend it, Lord, missing nothing, taking nothing for granted. I thank you, Lord, for the beautiful blessings and surprises that you are planning for me in this new day.

> Lord, help me to step into this new day and welcome it joyfully.
>
> Lord, help me to step into myself and do this day's work caringly.
>
> Lord, help me to step into the mystery of this new day expectantly.
>
> Lord, help me to enjoy all of this new day thankfully.
>
> Lord, help me to live each "precious present" moment of this new day carefully.

So the running of this new day has begun. Lord, run with me through this new day and make it good! *Amen.*

An Evening Psalm

So we have come to the ending of another day that began as this new day.
The day is over. Classes are done. Night has come. We prepare for rest and sleep.

We quiet ourselves. We are still, inside and outside. We listen. Our thoughts ebb and flow. We let the day's happenings pass in review:

Something good that happened comes to mind,
An appreciation reaffirms, a surprise registers,
A sharing lingers, an idea emerges,
A quieting is felt.

Quiet time. Come to the quiet. Be in stillness. Be at rest. Unclog cluttered minds. Let the busy world be stilled. Let the fever of life be over. Let there be peace at last.

Be receptive to a sustaining presence. Be quieted, resting and being held and nurtured in strong, yet gentle, arms that encircle, enfold and hug:

A heavenly Mother holding each and all . . .
A heavenly Father letting each and all rest against strong knees . . .

A Cord communion community becomes a holding place of safety, security, trust.

Cord community . . . a faith community in the midst of transition and change and journeys to far countries and promised lands.

Cord community . . . surrounded with love and hope, nourished now with bread and wine.

Cord community . . . sharing, receiving, renewing, communing.

Cord community . . . a Mother and Father God holding, nurturing, sustaining, strengthening and enfolding one and all under the shadow of holy, gentle wings.

Cord community . . . listening at the end of the day to the praying of an evening psalm as it is sung by John Michael Talbot:

In the quiet I have stilled my soul
    like a child at rest on its mother's breast.
Just come to the quiet. Come and still your soul
    like a child at rest on its daddy's knee.
Come and still your soul completely.

Run with Perseverance

*Let us run with perseverance the race that is set before us, looking to
Jesus the pioneer and perfecter of our faith, who for the sake of the joy
that was set before him endured the cross . . . . Consider him who endured . . .
so that you may not grow weary or lose heart.*
— Hebrews 12:1-3

It was a game that started with such excitement and intensity. The Cobbers scored and released cheering freshmen from the bondage of their beanies. Things seemed so hopeful and promising. Then things begin to change. Momentum went over to the Dragons, and the Cobbers had to dig in and hang on. Play after play they hung in there, toughed it out and persevered. They willed themselves to keep at it, enduring, persisting, playing with determination and heart. They persevered, believing they could do it. And they did.

Orientation, too, had started with such excitement, so much energy and activity. Then, two weeks into classes, things began to change. The dog days of September were upon us. The exhilaration of new beginnings and returnings gave way to fatigue and lethargy. The momentum had bogged down. It was time to hang in there and tough it out, one day at a time, one class at a time, one assignment at a time, one meeting at a time. "Shoulds" overwhelmed. Procrastination tempted.

The exciting race of the school year turned into a plod. It was time to settle in and persevere in the long marathon of the semester. What began so optimistically and dramatically now has become a relentless daily grind.

What is needed to get through these dog days of September? The text suggests "perseverance" and "endurance":

. . . hard-headed determination, resilient tenacity,

. . . sustaining will power, consistent effort.

The text also suggests looking to Jesus as the example and model for persevering: ". . . for the sake of the joy that was set before him, he endured the cross." For the sake of what lay ahead, Jesus endured and persevered. "Consider him," the text suggests, "so that you may not grow weary or lose heart."

It's interesting that the text uses the word *heart* here. Persevering is one of the biblical words for heart. *Desire* is another biblical word for heart . . . so is *determination* . . . so is *direction* . . . so is *purpose* . . . so is *passion* . . . so is *guts*.

Just think of facing each day with that kind of persevering heart.
Just think of facing each day looking to Jesus as your role model.
Just think of facing each day with desire and determination, with
direction and purpose, with passion and guts!

So let's go! Let's press on! Let's run with perseverance!

A Crystal Gaze

Brand new season . . . Crystal Bowl!
Slay the Dragons . . . that's our goal!

Gazing into the Crystal Bowl, we truly believe that we can!
Let's play the game with **confidence!**
> Out on the field we find
> Success begins with our state of mind.
> We've got to believe in ourselves
> If we plan to rise to reach for the prize.

Let's follow the example of one who showed us how to win:

> Jesus modeled "possibility" and "power."
> Jesus said: "All things are possible to those who believe!"
> Jesus promised: "With God empowering us nothing is impossible!"

> For Jesus each person was a gold mine of possibility.
> Each person had the power to make a difference.
> Each person could decide the outcome of a situation.
> Each person could change the outcome of a game.
> Each player could become extraordinary.
> Each play could be a turning point.

Jesus committed himself to a God who empowered his power! You can too! You can do far more than you believe is possible. You can commit yourself to a God who will help you believe that.

Let's quiet ourselves now and be still. Let's be in prayer and ask God to come into our hearts and minds. Let's tell God what we need for today's game. Let's listen to God's answers. Let's ask God to come and be with our team now as we pray:

> *Help me to play today with possibility and with power.*
> *Help me to play with confidence and dedication.*
> *Help me to believe in myself and in my teammates.*
> *Help me to make things happen to decide the outcome.*
> *Help me to play with energy and skill, with intensity and will.*

> *I promise that my teammates can count on my doing my part.*
> *I dedicate myself to play the kind of game that can make a difference.*
> *I commit myself to unselfish teamwork and support.*
> *Give me such confidence and commitment that I can say as I play:*
> *"I'll let nothing deter or defeat us." Amen.*

A 'Whobody' Visit

The phone rings.
Grandma is on the line.
It's so good to hear her voice. I almost start to cry.
She and Grandpa are wondering how I'm doing at college.
She asks how I'm getting along with my roommate.
She wonders how the food is.
She asks if I'm eating enough and getting enough sleep.

Grandma says they've been thinking about me a lot and praying for me. They're so excited for me to be here at Cord, she tells me. Grandma says they worry about me some and miss me a lot. She says they've called and called and only get a recording:

". . . can't come to the phone now. I'm at the library studying . . ."

Grandma says I must really be getting smart, studying so much. Then she asks if I have anything planned for the weekend. She and grandpa are wondering:

Would I mind if they came to visit me?
Would I have the time?
They wouldn't want me to miss too much studying.
They'd just like to see me and find out how I'm doing.

Would I have the time! I almost scream out loud, I'm so happy.
"Please come!" They're "whobodies," and have they ever made my day!
When they come, I show them my very clean, neat room. I introduce them to my roommate and all my new "whobody" friends. Grandma and Grandpa are so happy for me.
Then Grandma sees that theme lying on top of my desk, next to the printer. She picks it up, looks at it, pages through it and then says to me: "Did you write this paper all by yourself? Wow! That looks like a masterpiece! Tell me about it."
Grandpa doesn't say much. He just sits there and smiles . . . and remembers. He has a great memory. Everything anyone says reminds him of something. He's so neat and sweet. I just love him, and so do my friends.
Grandpa and Grandma give me a "whobody" weekend. They take me shopping at West Acres. They take me to dinner. When they leave, Grandpa slips me a twenty-dollar bill.
Thanks, Grandpa and Grandma, for being "whobodies" when I needed you so. I don't even mind getting back to studying after you've left. I feel so loved and special. I feel like God has answered my prayers.
God has sent me Grandpa and Grandma as "whobody" angels.

Risk Taking a Chance

It was such an unbelievably beautiful rosebush . . . deep red roses brilliant in the morning sunshine, their smell intoxicating and permeating, a heavenly surrounding of color and fragrance. I wanted to capture and keep that moment of beauty and that promise of blossoming. I wanted to bloom and grow like that rosebush.

Then I looked more closely. I noticed one tall rose stem with a large bud. The bud, still green, was drooping, unopened, not blossoming. It had a strong, living stem and a full, greening bud. Yet, it wasn't opening. This "deadhead" rose was drooping on its live stem, not fulfilling its potential, not living up to its possibility.

There have been times in my life when I have been like that "deadhead" rose. There have been times when I have been afraid to take the chance of opening up and blossoming. I've been afraid to blossom the way I can because it wouldn't be good enough, or as good as someone else's. I've been afraid at times to really be that rose that is uniquely me. I have memories of being taken for granted and feeling unappreciated when I opened up and blossomed. So I withdrew within myself, rather than risking another chance. I didn't believe in myself.

Jesus once described a similar situation: "As people think in their hearts, so they are!"

The way I think about myself, or something, creates the way I feel about myself or that situation. And the way I feel about myself affects the way I believe about myself. And the way I believe about myself affects the attitude I have toward myself and others . . . and the way I do or don't do things.

If I tend to think like that deadhead rose, I will tend to live life and do things anxiously, timidly and hesitantly. I will be afraid to take a chance and risk blossoming. I'll be afraid to do my best. I'll settle for less than what I am capable of doing.

When I let myself be like the blossoming rose, however, I will look on the positive side and see through the perspective of possibilities and opportunities. I'll claim the promise: *"With God all things are possible! I can do all things through Christ who gives me the strength to do them."* I'll claim the attitude the Apostle Paul had. Let me paraphrase what he said: *"Whatever happens to me, whatever situation I find myself in, I'll find a way to use it for something good!"*

So I'll take the chance and blossom. I'll have hopes and dreams that God *". . . is able to accomplish abundantly far more than all we can ask or imagine."* — Ephesians 3:20 I'll commit myself to giving it my very best. My believing that I can and my will that I can are as important as my skills. I'll dare to blossom and grow . . . bloom and grow . . . forever.

Two possibilities . . . two options: a deadhead rose or a blossoming rose! Dare to risk! Take a chance!

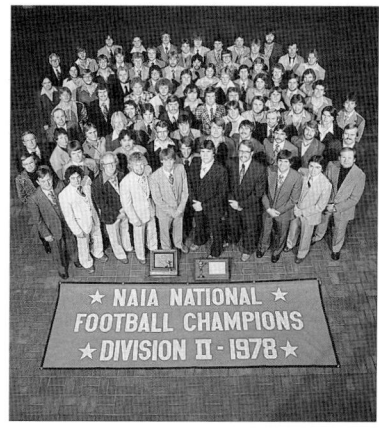

That Special Championship Season

Look at them, Lord.
See the players and coaches of our championship teams.
Call off their names, Lord.

Give to each of them the reward of work well done and honors won:
    . . . of recognition earned and thanks deserved,
    . . . of a place of honor here at Cord,
    . . . of the honor of your presence,
    . . . of impossible dreams becoming possible dreams.

Lord, you were near them throughout their championship seasons.

You were near them when they worked out and practiced:
    . . . when they played and performed,
    . . . when they won and when they lost,
    . . . when they won the final prize.

You were near them in caring, supportive, affirming teammates:
    . . . in coaching help and mentoring,
    . . . in families and friends who faithfully followed,
    . . . in all who cheered and encouraged them on.

Give to each team member joy and satisfaction in their accomplished dream.
Let all of them know that their contributions made a difference. "We can do it" was their goal as they played with passion and soul.
    Thank you that "hearts were in harmony" for a total team effort.
    All hail to you, team members — Concordia honors you and thanks you for that special championship season!

We Dedicate This Building

Lord, you have done marvelous things, and we will praise you!

> For gifts that build buildings and put students in them,
> For builders that put them together and workers that maintain them,
> For teachers that open doors to knowledge and truth in them,
> For students who emerge thoughtful and informed through them.

Lord, you have done marvelous things, and we will praise you!

> For ministry through giving and administering,
> For ministry through building and maintaining,
> For ministry through teaching and learning,
> For ministry through study and dedication.

Lord, you have done and are doing marvelous things, and we will praise you!

We will praise you for all who, in this new building, will:

> . . . harness talent and paraphrase history,
> . . . interpret issues and research unknowns,
> . . . create ideas and unlock mystery.

Lord, you have done and are doing marvelous things, and we will praise you!

All your works praise you, O Lord, and your faithful servants bless you! Your gifts are many, and in wisdom you made all things to give you glory!

> Blessed and dedicated be this building to your praise and honor.
> Grant that this building may be a place where your will is done.
> May all that is done within its walls glorify your name.

Lord, you have done and are doing marvelous things, and we will praise you!

A Psalm of Relaxation

Sit back in your chairs. Sit quietly. Be still.
Begin to let go of the day's activities. Let go of work and worries.
Breathe deeply and easily. Let yourself get comfortable.
Let your body begin to relax. Let your mind begin to let go of
    cluttered thoughts.
Think of the word *calm*. Take some calming breaths.

Open your hands.
Open yourself to Jesus coming to calm you and give you peace.
Let his presence calm you. Let his peace quiet you.
Relax! Let go! Let God's peace flow into you.
Breathe in God's peace. Breathe in God's calm.

Feel yourself held and calmed in God's arms.
Feel your whole body being relaxed by God's peace.

Feel yourself going deeper and deeper into Jesus' care.
Feel yourself going deeper and deeper into quieting prayer.

Jesus is asking you to give him all your worries and cares.
Jesus is asking you to give him all your fears and your fatigue.
Jesus is asking you to relax and let go in him, and be at peace.

Feel God taking your burdens and anxiety, your tiredness and stress.
Feel God's peace like a sponge soaking up all your tension.
Feel God's peace in your mind and in your heart.
Feel God's peace in your body and in your breathing.
Feel God's peace relaxing and surrounding you.

You feel God's presence as you wait, calmed and quieted.
You come as a child, open and expectant, to partake of bread and wine.
You come with open hands to receive: "Given and shed for you!"

You return to your chairs thankful for the touch and taste of God's love.
You leave peaceful and quieted, sharing God's peace and yours.
You go in peace to serve the Lord.

Kyrie! Heal!

How powerful, how healing, how comforting, how strengthening Jesus' touch must have been. Just think of it:

>. . . children, blessed and held in loving arms,
>>. . . a blind person's eyes anointed, seeing,
>>>. . . a leper, cured,
>>>>. . . a lame person, walking,
>>>>>. . . a disciple sinking, rescued,
>>>>>>. . . tired feet, washed,
>>>>>>>. . . bread and wine, promising.

Tonight in this Wednesday-night Communion and service of healing, Jesus is present to touch and heal. "Take and eat," he invites, "take and drink; it is I. I'll satisfy!" And we come with open hands to take our gifts from his own hands, and we are blessed.

Then, having received bread and wine from his hands we receive his touch. Fragrant oil and the sign of the cross anoint our foreheads. Words of promise are spoken: "I anoint you with oil so that you may know the healing power of Christ's love."

Jesus' touch, in bread and wine, is mine! Jesus' touch, in oil and sign, is mine! For me . . . personally!

> *Some of us are hurting tonight and need a healing touch.*
> *Some of us are anxious tonight and need a reassuring touch.*
> *Some of us are uncertain tonight and need a reaffirming touch.*
> *Some of us are happy tonight and need a thankful touch.*
>
> *Lord of presence, God of touch, reach us when we need you much.*
> *Shield us when we face too much, heal us with your gentle touch.*

As we leave this Communion having experienced Jesus' touch in bread and wine, in oil and sign, we reach out and touch and share God's peace that means so much.

Unexpected Interruptions

I was running late all that hectic October day.
I had overscheduled myself with meetings and appointments.
People were dropping in unexpectedly needing "just a minute."
Phone calls were piling up; coffee breaks were interrupted.

I had already called Ann to let her know I would be late for dinner. With relief, I finally shut off the lights and was heading out the door. There greeting me was someone pleading: "I really need to see you right now. It can't wait!" So there it was . . . another interruption among so many unexpected ones that day.

Unexpected interruptions were quite common for Jesus. His busy days and schedules are constantly being interrupted. While he is on his way to a scheduled appointment, he gets interrupted with unexpected demands. While he is responding to that interruption, he is interrupted with a second one. So he puts the first interruption on hold while he responds to the more immediate one.

I sense that Jesus is telling me something about ministry here. His ministry seemed to be full of unexpected interruptions. I often wonder if ministry isn't a story of continual, unexpected interruptions. Unplanned situations come up that have an urgency about them. Unexpected emergencies demand immediate attention.

Rather than being frustrated by these interruptions, it seems that Jesus flowed with them and turned them into unexpected and surprising blessings. It gave him the opportunity to meet people he hadn't expected to meet, to teach lessons he hadn't planned on teaching, and to do healings he had not planned on doing. Interruptions became opportunities for new possibilities of ministry.

I wonder what Jesus thinks as he looks at our busy schedules. Is it possible he delights in disrupting them with unexpected interruptions? He'll probably take us on unplanned detours on our daily trips. He'll insert into our already crowded days timeouts and 'tweeners that will demand our immediacy and attention. He'll send emergencies that cry with urgency.

As we press on with our busy daily schedules these October days, remember that things may not proceed as we have planned. We need to be open to Jesus interrupting and detouring us. We need to take those occasions and use them as opportunities of blessing. We need to let Jesus take us on ventures of which we cannot see the ending, on paths as yet untraveled, through interruptions for opportunities unknown.

On Taking a Break

*And on the seventh day God finished the work that he had done.
So God blessed the seventh day and hallowed it, because on it God rested from all the work he had done.*
— Genesis 2:2-3

What a marvelous example God gave us for taking a break!

After six days of intensive work and amazing creativity, God took the seventh day off to rest. After six days of intensive work, God set aside the seventh day and did nothing but rest. Not only did God take a whole day off, God also blessed and hallowed the day to be a day of rest.

We've been through a block of nonstop activity and creativity too! Not only did we fill up our weekdays with intensive work and activity, we also filled up our weekends the same way. We did not set aside any "seventh" days for rest and taking breaks. We did not observe or hallow the "seventh" day. It's no wonder that we're getting tired and running out of gas and getting sick.

God was smarter. God was exhausted by the seventh day. God knew it. God knew what was needed — a day off, to rest. And God cared for those personal needs by making the Sabbath a day of rest. If God needed to rest, then we know we do too! Our bodies are trying to tell us that. Stuffed sinuses, sore throats and runny noses are sending us a message about taking a break.

God didn't wait for a cold to have permission to rest. God rested even when there was still some energy left. And you know . . . God not only had energy to take a break and rest, God also had energy left over to celebrate and to take stock.

After work, God rested. After work, God played.

After working, and resting, and playing, God took stock again. God took some time during the day of rest to sort things out. Then God could go into Monday with a clearer perspective and purpose and plan. Then God could go into a new week with renewed energy and enthusiasm and effectiveness.

God gives us a marvelous example for our life and work here . . . the rhythm of a "One-in-Seven Principle": **six days to work . . . then one day set aside for rest, play and taking stock . . . then back to work again in a new week, renewed, refreshed, replenished, restored.**

God gives us that example for taking a break this weekend:

. . . some work, probably . . . some catching up, hopefully!
. . . some working ahead, possibly . . . some rest, definitely!
. . . some play, naturally . . . some taking stock, decidedly!

Let God hallow and bless our break. We really do deserve a break this weekend!

Praying Goodbyes

"Oh, only for so short a while have you loaned us to each other," notes an ancient Aztec Indian prayer.

>Fall comes and summer ends.
>Leaves turn red and golden.
>Trees say goodbye to summer foliage.
>Geese say goodbye to northern summers.
>
>Endings come and goodbyes come.
>Sometimes they come sooner — unexpectedly and unplanned for.
>A casual "goodbye," "have a good day," "see you tomorrow"
>Becomes an unplanned, final goodbye.

There is a rhythm in our lives, so taken for granted, about endings and beginnings, goodbyes and hellos, leavings and homecomings. Sometimes that rhythm is changed unexpectedly with a death:

>. . . a student suddenly gone,
>. . . a parent suddenly gone,
>. . . a grandparent suddenly gone,
>. . . a colleague and friend suddenly gone.

What we assumed to be a "see you again soon" is gone. What we took for granted as the normal goodbye and hello ritual is gone. We realize in such a hurting and profound way about our relationships and life: "Oh, only for so short a while have you loaned us to each other."

Suddenly we realize that we don't have all the time in the world. We can't take tomorrow for granted. Life is a gift. Each day is a gift. People are gifts — special, yet fragile and perishable. Every meeting on any given day is a gift, never to be taken for granted. Every greeting is an exchange of gifts, gifts of God to each other and for each other.

We have come together in this All Saints worship to say our goodbyes and to pray our goodbyes for some special saints who have left us so unexpectedly. As we pray our goodbyes, we ask God to give us another opportunity, another chance, to live each day to the fullest.

We will let nothing go unfinished. We will live each day missing nothing. We will say the loving, caring, affirming, appreciative words to each other daily. We will say our hellos and goodbyes more meaningfully. We will not assume anything about tomorrow other than to know that God's love will rise before the sun.

Oh, only for so short a while have you loaned us to each other!

Thank You

*For atoms and ants, for art and amazement,
   for your assurance and answers . . . we thank you, Lord.*

*For blood banks and butterflies, for books and beauty,
   for your bounty and blessing . . . we thank you, Lord.*

*For creation and conversation, for children and carols,
   for your compassion and care . . . we thank you, Lord.*

*For food and families, for freedom and fun,
   for your friendship and favor . . . we thank you, Lord.*

*For harvests and health, for hope and harmony,
   for your healing and help . . . we thank you, Lord.*

*For laughter and love, for listening and learning,
   for your loving and liberating . . . we thank you, Lord.*

*For possibilities and peace, for preludes and poetry,
   for your presence and promises . . . we thank you, Lord.*

*For seasons and sleep, for song and sharing,
   for your shepherding and serving . . . we thank you, Lord.*

Have Mercy

Lord have mercy . . . Christ have mercy . . . Lord have mercy

    . . . for the poor. O Lord, provide for them through us.
    . . . for the homeless. O Lord, shelter them through us.
    . . . for the lonely. O Lord, befriend them through us.
    . . . for the grieving. O Lord, comfort them through us.

Lord have mercy . . . Christ have mercy . . . Lord have mercy

    . . . for the despairing. O Lord, give them hope through us.
    . . . for the frightened. O Lord, reassure them through us.
    . . . for the hungry. O Lord, feed them through us.
    . . . for the refugees. O Lord, give them a new start through us.

Lord have mercy . . . Christ have mercy . . . Lord have mercy

    . . . for the doubting. O Lord, give them faith through us.
    . . . for the struggling. O Lord, give them encouragement through us.
    . . . for the victims. O Lord, surround them through us.
    . . . for the anxious. O Lord, give them a new perspective through us.

Lord have mercy . . . Christ have mercy . . . Lord have mercy

    . . . for those serving. O Lord, support them through us.
    . . . for those seeking. O Lord, respond to them through us.
    . . . for those succeeding. O Lord, rejoice with them through us.
    . . . for those sent forth. O Lord, surround them with love and hope through us.

Kyrie . . . Kyrie . . . Kyrie Eleison!

Slow Down

We're heading north from Pittsburgh on I-79. Four lanes of traffic at 60 mph, bumper-to-bumper, tractor-trailers, trucks, vans, buses, sports cars, passenger cars . . . all driving like there is no tomorrow.

In the front seat, $3^{1}/_{2}$-year-old granddaughter, Michelle, looks around at everyone . . . at Mom and Dad, and little brother, and at her grandparents. Then with childlike delight, she announces: "We're all together now!"

In the back seat, $1^{1}/_{2}$-year-old grandson, Mark, has fallen asleep in his car seat, his head resting gently against his mother's arm and shoulder. All around him there is the noise of frantic speed: squealing brakes, honking horns, the roar of traffic, tires slapping against rough concrete, suicidal drivers crossing lanes to get to opposite lane exits, drivers driving up the backs of cars ahead of them, seemingly desperate to get to their destinations, in the shortest possible time.

None of this disturbs the gently sleeping Mark as he sleeps trusting and quieted on his mother's arm.

As I watch the scene from the front seat, I recall a verse paraphrased from Psalm 131:

> *"I have calmed and quieted my soul like a child quieted in its mother's arms. Like a child that is quieted is my soul."*

I think to myself: "That's what I need right now. That's what I need to pray for: To trust God the way Mark is trusting and resting beside his mom. I need to trust and rest in God that way!"

Since coming back from fall break into all the hectic, frantic activity here, I have thought of that freeway scene. Our days are like driving that busy interstate:

> . . . bumper-to-bumper activity,
> . . . meetings and committees and schedules crowding us,
> . . . tailgating each other in the rush to get somewhere,
> . . . charging ahead in the fast lane, frustrated,
> . . . activities crowding, deadlines pushing, commitments fatiguing.

What we need now is to get out of this heavy traffic. We need to get off the frenzied freeway we're on. We need to slow ourselves down. We need to pace ourselves. We need to take some breaks — get some rest. We need to deliberately set some time aside in order to quiet ourselves. We need to lean against God, as Mark leaned against his mother, and feel safe enough to let go and fall asleep and rest.

"I have calmed and quieted my soul, like a child quieted in its mother's arms."

Simple Gifts

Psalm 23.
The most-believed Psalm of all.
Simple language.
Simple gifts.
Humble images . . . profound meanings:

>. . . childlike trust,
>>. . . safety and protection,
>>>. . . promise and presence,
>>>>. . . surrounding and nurture.

Simple, powerful words of our own experiencing:

>. . . concern and caretaking,
>>. . . community and communion.

A song that sings about six simple basic daily needs:

>. . . peace,
>>. . . promise,
>>>. . . presence,
>>>>. . . provisions,
>>>>>. . . protection,
>>>>>>. . . plenty.

Six short, simple, profound, powerful attributes of my life,
Ending in a doxology of God's goodness,
Spreading a bountiful banquet table in the midst of my vulnerability,
Inviting me to places of rest and refreshment.

Simple, essential gifts for my daily journey.

The Lord is my shepherd.
I will never be in want.
My deepest needs are met.
Beside restful waters I am led.
In the pasture of plenty my soul now lies down.

Don't Just Do Something!

It surprises you with the suddenness of its coming.
Suddenly it's Advent and you're off and running.
Shopping days are already counting down.
Decorations are already coming up.
The frantic finishing of assignments and papers is beginning.
Christmas Concert rehearsals are under way.
Advent has barely begun, yet Christmas is in full swing.

You wait for the Christmas Concert to help you prepare.
You want to hear the music that tugs and caresses heartstrings and memory.
You long to sing the familiar carols of childlike faith and wonder.
You wait to hear instruments and choirs bringing you heavenly music.
You wait to be where only a song can say what Christmas means.

"In the Shadow of Your Wings" blazes out into the darkened auditorium.
Hundreds of voices bring the consolation of holy wings spread gently over you.

Stand There!

You join your voice in carol song:

> *Here let all, great and small*
> *Kneel in awe and wonder . . .*

Advent's invitation about Christmas is to do nothing but be quiet,
Advent's invitation about Christmas is to do nothing but receive.

Don't just do something! Stand there!
Stand there at the manger, quietly adoring and eagerly waiting!

Stand there at the manger with your arms outstretched.
Stand there at the manger to receive God's most precious gift.
Stand there at the manger holding to your heart your Savior.

Don't just do something! Stand there!

Things That Make for Christmas Peace

So much of the Christmas story talks about peacefulness and draws us away from violence. So much of the Christmas story suggests quietness and draws us away from noise.

That first Christmas night, the noise of the busy world is hushed. The fever of the day's work is done. In that shed and manger bed, we are welcomed into quiet and peace:

> *How silently, how silently the wondrous gift is given.*
> *The world in solemn stillness lies.*

Christmas . . . quietness! peacefulness! a baby! So easy to receive. So special to hold. So comforting with promise: "Do not be afraid!"

This is how God comes at Christmas . . . as a vulnerable child who is announced by lamplight and silence, and then by singing and quieting words: "Do not be afraid!" God comes to us as a child who does not make us afraid.

In a world of violence and victims, and anger and aggression, God comes gently and peacefully, quietly and vulnerably, as a child. God comes to bless and not to hurt, to give and not to take. God comes to still our hurried, hectic, hurting lives with quieting peacefulness.

That's why we love Christmas so! That's why we yearn for Christmas so! We love and long for that Christmas story that offers us and our world again the good news that God is bringing us and our world the gift of peace, wrapped in the swaddling clothes of a child born in a manger.

We yearn again this Christmas for quietness and peacefulness. We yearn again this Christmas for the gift of a child bringing peace. We yearn again for angels singing:

> *"Peace on earth, good will to all!"*

We yearn again for Magi to be led by the guiding of a star to bring precious, life-giving gifts to all the needy children of the world.

We yearn again this Christmas for the good news that God through the child Jesus will bring us and our world the gift of peace. A weary world toiling beneath life's crushing load, resting beside weary roads, also yearns to hear *the glorious song of old, from angels bending near the earth: 'Peace on earth, good will to all, from heaven's all-gracious king.'*

We yearn again this Christmas for the wonderfully sweet, consoling, comforting words of angels to a world fitfully toiling with slow and painful steps: *"Don't be afraid. I bring you good news of a great joy!"*

We yearn again this Christmas to be people of peace responding in peaceful ways. We yearn in the midst of all our hopes and fears to become more like the child Jesus: to bless more and hurt less, to give more and take less, to think more of others and less of self, to take peace with us into our days and our deeds, and to let peace begin with us as we live more peaceful lives.

Peace and joy to you this Christmas
as you take peace, live peace and have peace!

Come Home with Me for Christmas

Home for Christmas! How you long for it right now! How you pray for it right now: "Jesus, come home with me for Christmas! Let me come home:

>   . . . to the familiar sounds and smells,
>   . . . to hugs and laughter, to food and sharing,
>   . . . to my own room and quiet when I need it,
>   . . . to family routines and rituals, to gatherings and activities,
>   . . . to gifts and giving,
>   . . . to old and special friendships renewed,
>   . . . to rest and rootedness, to home and family."

    Home for Christmas! How you long for it. How you pray for it: "Jesus, come home with me for Christmas! Jesus, give me a good scene at home this Christmas:

>   . . . let there be fun and laughter,
>   . . . let there be acceptance and appreciation,
>   . . . let there be respect and tolerance,
>   . . . let there be listening and openness,
>   . . . let there be encouragement and praise,
>   . . . let there be comfortableness and peacefulness."

    How you pray: *"Jesus, come home with me this Christmas!"* Some of you are keenly aware that Christmas won't be the same this year. A family member is missing. A place at the table is empty. You'll miss how that person made Christmas special for you and everyone at home. You'll miss a presence, a voice, a place. It just won't be the same Christmas without that person. So you pray: *"Jesus, come home with me this Christmas; be with our family and help us make it through."*

    Some of you pray: *"Jesus, come home with me this Christmas and let me feel more welcome! Please don't let there be the arguments and the yelling, and the silence and the coldness.* Please let there be some peace and pleasantness. Please, Jesus, let me feel like I still have a home and a place. I really know you know the meaning of *'there was no place for them in the inn.' Jesus, please come home with me this Christmas!"*

    Whatever your circumstances and situation and need, remember that Christmas means "Emmanuel — God is with you." You are not alone. So as you pray: *"Jesus, come home with me for Christmas,"* know that God will send you angels unaware and aware; hidden and compassionate; through parent and friend, brother and sister, neighbor and stranger; in shopping mall and church; in gift and giver; in work and worship — God will be coming to you. The Savior's birth is your promise and guarantee. Jesus will be home with you for Christmas.

DECEMBER

Through the Eyes of a Child

Come, O child Jesus, show us the way,
Steal into our busyness with strength for each day.
Come stand beside us, Emmanuel, please stay,
Come as host at this special meal, we pray.

If some are sad in the dark tonight,
Lord, draw them close in the candlelight.
If a heart is hurt and lonely tonight,
Pour out your balm and make it right.

If people tonight see no Christmas light,
Nor feel your love come down from the height,
Touch them and fill them with heavenly light,
And let them experience your saving might.

Let each of us know you are at our door,
And you promise you'll stay forevermore.
Steal into our studying with focus, we pray,
Stand close beside us and walk on our way.

Come as our dear friend this Christmas and stay,
And safely watch over us day after day.
Then, Lord, in turn, as our candles we raise,
We will respond with our gifts and our praise.

Magi and Graduates . . . Follow a Star

*You set a star in the heavens that the Magi followed on a faith journey.
By the light of that star, you led them to what they were seeking.*

*Set a star in the heavens that our graduating seniors can follow.
Guide them on their faith journey to careers and lives of service.*

*Your star led the way to the infant Savior.
There Magi offered him the best of their gifts.*

*Let that star guide these graduating seniors to Bethlehem too.
There let them offer you the best of their gifts.*

*Guide their journey now as they take their bearing from a star.
Send them into the world thoughtful and dedicated to the Christian life.*

*By the light of that star, take them on roads as yet untraveled.
Take them on ventures of which they cannot see the ending.*

*Let them know that your hand is leading them and your love is supporting them.
Magi and graduates . . . follow a star.*

The Magic Slate

The seconds tick down, one by one, as the countdown to midnight is chanted. Then suddenly it's midnight. The old year is over. The new year has begun.

It's a most wondrous moment. With one exhilarating and freeing "*zzzlippp*," the old year is peeled away and erased, like the clearing of a magic slate. Last year's mistakes are erased. The new year offers a clean, clear slate.

The new year is wonderful. It is so fresh and new, so clean and unblemished. The magic slate with one freeing and forgiving "*zzzlippp*" has opened the door to a fresh start in a new year.

"Give us this new year," we resolve. "We'll spend it, missing nothing."
"Give us this new year," we pray. "We'll take nothing for granted."

The minutes and hours of each day become a gift of opportunity and possibility. They are a perishable gift. Once spent, they are gone. Yesterday cannot be recalled or undone. Opportunities are used or wasted. Whether wise or unwise, good or bad, what is done is final. There is no refund, no exchange.

Only God with the gift of that magic slate of forgiveness can undo what we have done or failed to do. With that freeing "*zzzlippp*," God says:

I will forgive their iniquity, and remember their sin no more.
— Jeremiah 31:34

Transgressions and transactions are forgiven and forgotten. The gift of a new chance, a new opportunity, a new day is given. Yesterday is wiped clean. Each day is a fresh new start.

So we go into this new year and new semester resolving to live more passionately and compassionately and differently. We pray as we begin:

God, give us another year, another semester, another month, another week, another day, another hour, another chance, another opportunity, another gift. We will spend it, missing nothing. We will take nothing for granted. We will make it good.

*And God, when we soil and spoil your gifts of time and opportunity, we pray your forgiveness and forgetfulness. Send us the freeing **"zzzlippp"** of your magic slate to wipe clean, to blot out and to erase our mistakes.*

Here comes the new year and new semester with all its possibilities. They excite us and fill us with joy and wonder and thanks.

Blessed Are You

The Word for the New Year is "Blessed are the peacemakers!"

Blessed are you who take peace with you everywhere:
 . . . who take peace with you as you drive your cars,
 . . . who take peace with you into your work places,
 . . . who take peace with you into classroom and office.

Blessed are you who take peace with you everywhere:
 . . . who take peace with you into home and dorm,
 . . . who take peace with you into every meeting,
 . . . who take peace with you into practice and rehearsal,
 . . . who take peace with you into doing and correcting papers.

Blessed are you who take peace with you everywhere:
 . . . who take peace with you into word and deed,
 . . . who take peace with you into hellos and goodbyes,
 . . . who take peace with you into all your moments and days.

Blessed are you who take peace with you everywhere.

Take peace and be instruments of God's peace in this new year.

Blessed are you!

Magi Journey Eastward

Now when Jesus was born into the world in the days of Reagan and Gorbachev, the kings, behold, Magi came from the west to Russia saying: "Where are they all? We have seen a satellite in the east and we have heard a terrible news about an earthquake, and we have come to offer our help and our gifts."

When Gorbachev heard this news, he was glad, and all of Russia with him. They were overwhelmed with the outpouring of aid and care. Then assembling all the officials and agencies and organizations, they set out to do rescue and rehabilitation operations.

Then Gorbachev said to the Magi openly and pleadingly: "Go and search diligently for all the lost ones, and when you find them, bring me word, that together we can rescue and care for them."

When the Magi had heard the king, they speedily went on their way, flying heavily loaded jet transports with gifts. And lo, the satellite which they had seen in the east went before them 'til it came to rest over the place where the earthquake was.

When they saw the place, they were shocked beyond belief. Then going immediately to the places where they were needed, they began to offer their gifts:

> . . . the gold of specialists and money and equipment,
> . . . the frankincense of medicines and food and clothes,
> . . . the myrrh of trauma support and burial needs.

And suddenly there was with the Magi a multitude from earth's wide bounds and from ocean's farthest coast, streaming eastward, a countless host, coming to worship and bringing gifts of peace on earth and good will to all.

42 JANUARY

In Loving Memory

We cried and clung to one another.
We prayed and sang and tried to say goodbye.
We came to remember those beautiful students who had died too soon.
We surrounded each other with love and comfort.

No one expected that this would be their last Christmas and New Year.
They were too young to die.
They had so many years to live.
They had so many things yet to give.
They had so many dreams to dream.
They had so many stories to write.
They had so many possibilities to discover.

Now they are gone.
Shocking phone calls, endless nights, desperate prayers mark their leaving.
Memories flood in.
Tears come unexpectedly, sometimes softly, sometimes harshly.
Sadness numbs us; anger disturbs us.
Questions race through our minds, unanswered.
We laugh, then cry, as we remember.

We are not ready to say a final goodbye.
We need to say a hello again.
We want to think about them, talk about them, remember them.
We want to thank grieving families for sharing them with us.
We want to hold them to our hearts in loving memory.
We want to say things we didn't get a chance to say to them.
We want their families to know the difference they made for us here.

They were a special gift to us.
Their lights still shine through their memorial candles.
They remind us how precious the present is.
They remind us to be precious and beautiful gifts to each other.

We remember them and surround their families with our presence.
We entrust them to a God who was there to hear their borning cry.
We leave them with a God who has for them one more surprise.
We pray for their safekeeping:

> ***Jesus, keep them living in your fold. Amen.***

Morning and Evening

Morning Your eyes open before the alarm goes off.
You lie quietly, orienting yourself to awakening.
You pray: "Hello, God! Good morning, day!"
You gently think your way into the things you'll need to do today.
You pray your way into today.

Then you get up and perform your morning rituals.
You let the hot shower invigorate your body with cleansing energy.
You think prayer thoughts about making today a good day.
You invite God to walk with you into all that today will bring.

You choose some clothes that make you feel good.
You take some unhurried moments for quiet meditation and prayer.
You take time to eat a good breakfast.
You have begun the day gently and purposefully, in prayer.

You have a good day. You do well on that test. You do some good studying.
You have some quality time with your friends.
You have a good practice. You get some good exercise.
You get a good start on that paper, and you are relieved.

Evening You have done enough for today. You decide to stop.
You made it a good day. You feel more in control of things.
You begin to switch gears. You begin to slow yourself down gently.
You take some time for quiet as you meditate and reflect on the day.
You listen to a favorite CD and let the music take away your stress.

You think quieting and calming thoughts. You take calming breaths.
You picture in your mind a calming, peaceful, restful place.
You think about good things that happened today.
You think about unexpected surprises and compliments you received.
You think about persons who made your day more special.
You feel loved and accepted. You feel better about yourself.

You thank God for the good day you had.
You ask God for a restful, peaceful night of sleep.
You pull your favorite comforter around you and feel God surrounding you.
You think of a favorite Bible verse and childhood prayer.
Your eyes begin to close in trustful, restful sleep.

Come, Lord Jesus

*Like a lavish angel you come, Lord, with wondrous love
    spilling from your hand, dispensing favor,
    touching our lives with your healing presence.*

*Like a comforting counselor you come, Lord, with attentive ears
    listening to your children praying,
    sending power, sending love, sending grace.*

*Like a gracious host you come, Lord, with bread and wine
    nurturing us with sustaining love,
    promising us your precious presence.*

*Like a lover of my soul you come, Lord, with caring arms
    enfolding us with unconditional love,
    anchoring us in extravagant care.*

*Thank you, Lord, for your love and care
    so deep and wide, so high beyond all thought,
    so lavishly given, so never-ending. Amen.*

Are You Listening?

I watched them as they sat in my office. They seemed so far apart. They weren't listening to each other. They were getting frustrated. They were beginning to raise their voices because they were not understanding one another. They were starting to argue because they were not listening to each other. She was trying to tell him what she was feeling. He was trying to solve the problem before he understood what she was feeling.

I stopped them. I asked him to just listen. I asked her to tell him again what she was feeling. Then I asked him to tell her what he was hearing about what she was feeling. I asked him to ask her about things he wasn't understanding.

Suddenly she smiled, made eye contact with him, took his hand gently and said: "Honey, that's exactly how I feel. That's what I was trying to tell you. Thank you for making the effort to listen to what I was feeling. Thank you for not trying to solve something that I only wanted you to understand."

It was a moment of warmth and understanding. It was a soothing, holy, intimate moment between husband and wife. It was an "aha" moment of togetherness.

God is that kind of listener to us. God doesn't give advice or try to fix things. God doesn't say we don't or shouldn't feel what we are feeling. God listens. God accepts. God understands.

God gives us that gift of listening . . . listening to accept and to understand. In families, in marriages, between roommates, between parents and children, between counselor and counselee, between student and teacher . . . God gives us that gift and opportunity to listen, understand, accept and come together.

Are you listening? It's the tie that binds our hearts together in Christian love!

So we pray: *Lord, give us tender listening hearts. Let us do loving listening things that surprise even ourselves. And Lord, thank you for listening with ears always open, heart lovingly accepting, and arms welcoming and enfolding. Amen.*

I Wonder About...

Very little has been said about the victim in the parable of the Good Samaritan. Very little has been said about the innkeeper who provided the long-term convalescent care.

I wonder about them. What is it like to be the victim in need of help and care? What is it like to be the one entrusted to do the caretaking with only a verbal promise of payment?

I also wonder about what is the best way to be a Good Samaritan? What is the best way to minister and care for someone who has fallen on difficult times? What do I say? What don't I say? What do I do? What don't I do? How best can I help? How do I get myself out of the way so the focus can be on that person's feelings and needs? Can I make a commitment to stay with that person through their times of crisis and need?

I wonder about the Good Samaritan. Did he keep the promise to return and pay? Did he come back and visit and see how the victim was doing and what else the victim might be needing? Did the Good Samaritan follow up with after-care planning and help?

I really wonder about the innkeeper. The situation required more than just emergency care. After being stabilized and out of intensive care, the patient would need a long, slow, tedious, difficult time of rehabilitation and long-term care.

The innkeeper was expected to provide all this care, having only the word of the Good Samaritan about returning and paying. I wonder if the patient's family ever came to visit and offer help? What if neither family nor Good Samaritan could pay the huge hospital bill? The innkeeper was expected to keep providing the care even then. The innkeeper was in reality becoming the Good Samaritan.

Parallel stories to the parables have the innkeeper as the key person in the story. They have the innkeeper being a woman who is also the Good Samaritan. She is a Christ figure and symbol of all the Good Samaritans of the world, so many of whom have been women.

One thing about the parable is certain. The patient was now the neighbor, needing care, and the innkeeper had become the Good Samaritan.

I go back to wondering about the best way to be a Good Samaritan. Maybe it is by being like the innkeeper. And should I fall on difficult times, I would want some Good Samaritan to take me to that innkeeper.

48

FEBRUARY

Be My Valentine

What if Valentine's Day were a special day in the Church year? And what if the appointed text for the day were a paraphrase of John 1:

>*In the beginning was the Word . . . and each one of us is a word of God called to speak God to our world?*

Valentine's Day is about Christmas!

>*The Word becomes a human being and lives among us. Each of us is a word of God called to speak God!"*

Christmas again on February 14! Valentines as a word of God! Valentines being God's personal word to someone through us! Think of what Valentine's Day could mean if we used it that way.

What if we sent valentine greetings as God's personal word to someone? Think of sending someone a special valentine remembering today. As we write that note and send it, we do it with a prayer for that person. That person's day will be brightened by our personal word. He will be blessed when he knows he is remembered. She will thank as she knows she is prayed for.

We are the word of God speaking God to that person. We are a little Christ incarnate to that person. "Be my valentine," we say. "Be Christ to someone," we pray.

We are the word of God speaking God's love and care and remembering. What a difference a valentine like that can make for someone.

I think of those times I received that kind of valentine from someone. The opening words are almost always the same:

>"For some reason you have been on my mind lately . . ."
>"You have kept returning to my thoughts, and I'm praying for you."
>"For some reason I felt compelled to write and thank you . . ."
>"I'm calling because I've felt concern about you . . ."

These valentines have truly been a word of God to me from someone. They have come at those times when I needed to be reassured. They have come at depleted times when I needed to be surprised by thanks.

>*Be the word of God to someone today.*
>*Don't postpone. Don't procrastinate.*
>*Be someone's special valentine today!*

Mountaintops and Valleys

Just when we think we cannot stand one more stormy, wintry day something wondrous happens. Spring break is just a few days away. Thoughts turn from frozen tundra to sunny gulf shores and powder snow on mountain slopes. Thoughts turn to Habitat trips and helping in warmer climates. Thoughts turn to getting out of here in order to recharge depleted batteries. Thoughts turn to having transfiguration experiences away from the harsh winter and life in the Red River Valley.

Maybe it's no accident that "Transfiguration Sunday" in the church year comes just before our spring break.

Peter, James, John and Jesus need to get away, too. They go to a mountaintop place for an intensive retreat experience together. There they discover Jesus in all his divinity and humanity. There they grasp the scope of his ministry and Godness. It's an awesome moment. It's a beautiful moment. It's a mountaintop experience moment. And they want to hold onto it, keep it and stay there forever . . . with Jesus only! They don't want to go back down into their life and work in the valley.

But moments have a way of ending. The now becomes the then. Mountaintops lead back down into valleys. Intimacy gives way to reality. Jesus can't only be held onto in an intense mountaintop experience. Jesus has to be followed and lived down in the valleys of service and need.

That's the way it is in our faith journeys. We have our mountaintop experiences with Jesus, and then, with him, come back down and have our incarnational experiences with him in the valleys of life.

Mountain climbers say that often the most difficult part of a climb is the coming back down from the summit. It isn't easy to leave the heavenly and transcendent and come back down into the day-by-dayness of the valley.

I covet for you many mountaintop experiences and transfigurations this spring break. I wish you many moments for mountaintop living and transfigurations in your faith journeys. Then I wish you safe descents and returns down into the valley where you live responsibly and faithfully . . . and where you are glad for the valley and the gift of days, and people and opportunities.

May you have mountaintop experiences where you can say, "Lord it was good for us to be here," and may you have down-in-the-valley experiences where you also say, "Lord, it is good for us to be here."

LESSONS 51

Living Bible Verses

To Jesus, every person has the potential to make a difference.
To Jesus, every situation has the possibility for something positive.

You believe that too!
That's why more than 100 of you have volunteered.
You are "Habitat for Humanity" ministers on a mission of mercy.
You are here in chapel today to be commissioned for your trip.

Just think of the possibilities for good this spring break.
Just think of what you will be bringing in order to build.
You are bringing your particular Bible verse by your style of ministry.
You bring yourself as that passage into a specific situation.
You are the bringer, the bearer, the being, the builder of that verse.
Your work of bringing and building will make a house a home.

Be living Bible verses on this Habitat trip.
Be Christ's letters of recommendation.
Be little Christs.
Be escorts of God's word.
Bring and bear, be and do God's word through your building.

Lord, here we are, living Bible verses, little Christs:

> *take our minds and work through them,*
> *take our ears and listen through them,*
> *take our voices and speak through them,*
> *take our hearts and love through them,*
> *take our hands and build through them,*
> *take our gifts and work through them. Amen.*

Good Guilt

It started as a misunderstanding. You were both tired. You had had a frustrating, awful day. You said some cutting, hurtful, unfair things to each other. She responded with name-calling and tears. You responded with stony silence. You both leave angry, unspeaking and estranged.

You feel terrible. You feel so guilty. You keep wanting to blame her: "If it weren't for those names . . . ." You keep trying to justify your behavior: "All I said was . . . ." Your guilt eats away at you. You can't study . . . you can't concentrate. You have no peace. You keep seeing her face.

Finally you admit to yourself what you did. You take responsibility for what you said. Even though it's late, you call her. The phone has hardly rung before she answers. You blurt out that you are sorry.

The words are hardly out of your mouth before the same words come back to you. You talk your way back together.

Guilt . . . apology . . . remorse . . . repentance . . . reconciliation.

You experience being taken back and forgiven. You experience reconciliation and restoration. You say goodnight and go to bed and sleep in heavenly peace.

Your guilt was good. It was a gift. It warned of something you had done for which you were responsible. It alerted you to an injury you had done to one you loved. It focused on you as the author of that action. It made you experience pain and remorse. It kept nagging at you 'til you did something about it.

That's good guilt. That's guilt as gift and blessing, as guardian of your goodness. It made you the author of reconciliation.

The Psalmist knew about good guilt:

> *Happy are those whose transgression is forgiven.*
> *While I kept silence, my body wasted away through my groaning all day long . . .*
> *Your hand was heavy upon me; my strength was dried up . . .*
> *Then I acknowledged my sin to you,*
> *And I did not hide my iniquity . . .*
> *You forgave the guilt of my sin.*
> — Psalm 32:1-5

Encouraging Words

Lord, we confess the many ways we set ourselves up against each other in conflict:

    . . . we confess our angry and critical words,
    . . . we confess our blaming and entrapping words,
    . . . we confess our judging and discounting words.

Lord, forgive all the unpeaceful words that we speak against each other.

Lord, help us to listen more carefully before we speak:

    . . . help us to hear the feelings in back of the words,
    . . . help us to understand the needs in back of the feelings,
    . . . help us to hear the compliment in back of the complaint.

Lord, when angry and blaming words escalate and voices rise:

    . . . make us more patient in understanding,
    . . . make us more attentive in accepting,
    . . . make us more aware of the need to be heard.

Lord, make us instruments of your peace through our words:

    . . . make us able to speak words of hospitality and healing,
    . . . make us able to speak words of warmth and welcome,
    . . . make us able to speak words of acceptance and appreciation.

Lord, you spoke words of reconciliation from the cross:

    . . . help us to speak reconciling words to one another,
    . . . help us to say respectful words to one another,
    . . . help us to be encouraging words for one another. *Amen.*

Special Crosses

This is Jason's baptismal cross. I wore it when I baptized him on the shores of Lake Minnewaska. I marked him with the sign of that cross with the words:

> *"Jason, child of God, you have been marked with Christ's cross . . .*
> *Jason, may you know the power of Christ's healing love."*

This is Dan's ordination cross. I wore it the day I ordained him into the holy ministry. I held it before him as I gave him the ordination charge:

> *"Dan, let it be acclaimed, is ordained a minister . . . .*
> *He has Christ's authority to preach the Word,*
> *He has Christ's authority to administer the sacraments.*
> *He is called to serve God's people."*

This is Brianne's baptismal cross. It was a gift to me from her dad, my son. I gave my granddaughter that cross at her baptism, saying:

> *"Brianne, wear this cross proudly as a sign of who you are and whose you are."*

Today is Ash Wednesday and the beginning of another Lenten season. It is a time for more-than-usual devotion to God. It is a time for more-than-usual focusing on the cross.

"Lift high the cross," we sing, *"the love of Christ proclaim."* We focus on the cross, not only as symbol, but also as sacrifice. We are called to be living crosses and little Christs this Lent. We are called to live our faith active in love this Lent. We can be hidden and compassionate little Christs, angels unaware:

> . . . doing our Lenten Ingathering,
> . . . building Habitat homes,
> . . . volunteering at Dorothy Day and Churches United,
> . . . doing random acts of kindness,
> . . . serving through SOS projects.

There is another cross. It is my Lord's cross. It draws me to it. It asks me to lift it high. It asks me to live Christ's love.

Mommy! Daddy!

The day has become like night. There is no light. A storm is threatening. Something earth-shaking is taking place. There is one hanging on a cross. A mother and some friends keep vigil.

Out of the twilight of Calvary come the words of a childhood prayer:

"Mommy! Daddy! Father into your hands I entrust my spirit."

Jesus, as he dies, says words his mother taught him to pray when he was a boy. His mother listened to his bedtime prayer then, and she does the same now. Jesus entrusts himself to a parent's presence and safely goes to sleep.

The words of prayer learned in childhood stay deep in memory. They are there as a video, ready to be played, readily available. They are there as a computer disk, stored and ready to be accessed. They are there in time of need to draw on for comfort and safety.

That's what is happening now for Jesus. He is hurting and feels so alone. He feels forsaken and abandoned. Then he looks down and sees his mother there, and he remembers. He remembers his childhood home at bedtime. He remembers his mother there, listening to his evening prayers. He remembers his mother kissing him goodnight, then tucking him in. He remembers saying with his mother:

"Father, into your hands I entrust my spirit."

Jesus doesn't feel so alone now. His mother is there with him. His father is there with him. He hasn't been abandoned. The words his mother taught him come unbidden to his lips. It's just like when he was a child, weary from play, wanting sleep. His mother is there and his father is there, listening to his prayer. He can safely go to sleep now.

"Mommy! Daddy! Abba! Into your hands I entrust my spirit."

That's a child's prayer prayed in a universal language. It rings out in the midst of terror, vulnerability and dying. It's the plaintive cry of a mortally wounded soldier. It's a child's cry of yearning for a parent's presence.

Jesus, feeling forsaken, sees his mother there beside him. Jesus, remembering, prays his bedtime prayer of trust to Abba, Father. They are both there with him . . . Mommy and Daddy! It's safe to say goodnight and go to sleep.

See you in the morning! Easter morning!

in the beginning
the breath of life
Resurrection + and the Life
born of water and the spirit

Mary! Martha!

Lord, we confess that we are often like Mary . . .

    We shirk mundane, everyday chores and duties.
    We choose what we and some consider more important.

Lord, we confess that we are often like Martha . . .

    We complain when we feel unappreciated and used.
    We blame when we feel neglected and stuck with "gofer" work.

    Like Mary, we may make so much "space for grace" that we neglect relationships and routine chores.

    Like Martha, we may get so busy with duties and detail that we are distracted from "making space for grace."

Lord, we ask for a better perspective and focus this Lenten season:

    to both make "space for grace" and tend to our daily duties,
    to ask for help without apology or complaint,
    to volunteer and serve with willingness and joy,
    to affirm what both Mary and Martha see as important,
    to maintain a balance and focus in everything we do.

Lord, lead us into a Mary! Martha! Lenten Season:

    Give us both "space for grace" and willing service.
    Let each day be filled with blessings and accomplishments.
    Let there be spiritual growth and personal giving.
    Let nothing distract us from choosing both worship and service. *Amen.*

Extravagant Love

There was this woman who loved Jesus very much.
Jesus had done so much for her and meant so much to her.
She wanted to do something special for him in return.

There was a man named Simon who also loved Jesus very much.
Jesus had healed him from life-threatening leprosy.
Jesus had been invited for an appreciation dinner.
It's Wednesday of Holy Week, in the Jerusalem suburb of Bethany.

During the after-dinner conversation, this woman sees an opportunity to act. She has been one of many hanging out around the courtyard, eavesdropping. "It's now or never," she thinks, as she crashes the party and pours a whole jar of expensive perfumed oil on Jesus.
    The people there, and especially the disciples, react with shock and anger. "Why this waste?" they say. "This oil could have been sold for a large amount of money and given to the poor." The disciples couldn't comprehend this woman's extravagant gift. They couldn't cope with her impulsive action. They couldn't understand how much her caring gift had meant to Jesus.
    Jesus understood her caring act and her extravagant gift. He accepted her act and gift and praised her for it. "You'll always have opportunity to help the poor," he said, "but you won't always have the opportunity to care for me. She has done a beautiful thing for me," Jesus continued; *"she has prepared me for burial, and what she has done will be remembered about her."* — Matthew 26:10-13 paraphrased

    This is the kind of giving that delights the heart of Jesus.
    It is a love that doesn't stop to calculate how much to offer.
    It is a love that finds and uses moments of opportunity.
    It is a love that is impulsive in action.
    It is a love that receives as well as gives.
    It is a love that lingers in memory.
    It is a love that gives specialness to persons.

What about our response to this kind of extravagant love?

This Lent let's dare to lay at the altar our own extravagant love!

60 APRIL

An Aloha Easter Experience

It's Easter morning, before dawn. Ann and I are at Wailea Beach on the island of Maui. We are on our way with hundreds of other tourists to the Easter sunrise service. The fragrance of tropical flowers fills the air. Palm trees and banyan trees wave gently. We are headed for a spot where the ocean will be at our backs and Mt. Haleakala will be to our front. We will have a choice seat to view the Easter sunrise coming up over Mt. Haleakala.

There is an expectancy and a hush all around. It seems like everyone and even creation itself is waiting and watching. Even the gulls have stopped their flights and sit quietly facing the coming sunrise.

Suddenly the sun seems to jump up over Mt. Haleakala. It's like we're standing on holy ground. "Christ is Risen!" chants the celebrant. Hundreds of voices respond: "Christ is risen, indeed!" The sunshine and God's "sonshine" are inviting us to resurrection and renewal. Then hands are joined in a deeply moving hymn of faith and hope: "Hawaii Aloha." We have had an unforgettable worship experience of an "Aloha" Easter sunrise.

Later that day, we fly to Oahu and have an Easter dinner with our hosts, Dan and Sue. Monday we head back to the remaining days of the semester. It's on the flight home that I become aware of a profound new meaning about the Easter we had just experienced.

The meaning of Easter became real not only through the message "He is risen," but also through messengers bringing the message. Easter became real to the disciples only when Jesus came to them personally. I realized that, too, on my flight home. Jesus had come to me personally through my Easter people. Dan and Sue were Easter people for me that Easter Sunday in Hawaii. There were hundreds of people back at the college who were Easter people for me. They had sent Ann and me on an all-expenses-paid trip as a thank-you for 25 years of ministry at Concordia.

What a very special Aloha Easter we were given. How thankful we were for all the Easter people who made Christ's resurrection presence real to us.

I became aware of one more message from Easter when classes began again. My task now was get back to work and be an Easter person with the Easter message.

A Prayer for Spring

Take me out of winter's cold prison.
Bring me out of hibernation.
Let spring come into my wintered body.
Let me feel warmth again, hope again, life again.

Breathe your spring spirit into my lethargy.
Blow over the fences of my self-pity.
Whisk away the blinders of my depression.
Sweep away my stale habits, my low opinion of myself.

Pull me together with an inner equilibrium.
Recharge and jump-start my drained, depleted battery.
Give me higher octane for driving in the fast lane.
Hold me steady under demands and deadlines before Easter.

Awaken me to the wonder of the sun's energizing light.
Make something new blossom and grow in my perspective.
Let the promise of spring sow seeds of optimism.
Make crosswinds blow up into resurrection showers.

Let the springtime wind melt winter snows.
Let the green of new life and promise appear.
Send forth from within me new shoots, fresh buds.
Awaken spring in Easter's resurrection symphony.

Going the Extra Mile

Lord, we're honoring some very special people tonight . . . ***our support staff.***

They truly make Concordia a place where hearts and hands work in harmony. Their work is another way of praying and saying *Soli Deo Gloria!*

Lord, thank you for our support staff:

> . . . thank you for their going the extra mile,
> . . . for doing the extra work,
> . . . for giving the extra word,
> . . . for making the extra effort,
> . . . for putting in the extra time.

Thank you for the way they make Concordia a special place to live and work.

Thank you for all the ways they serve and give:

> . . . for all the ways they maintain and repair,
> and tend and clean,
> and keep order in offices,
> and meet the people,
> and handle complaints,
> and answer phones,

> . . . for all the ways they keep the records,
> and sort the mail,
> and build and repair,
> and plant and paint,
> and keep us warm or cool,
> and take loaves and fish and feed thousands.

Thank you for all the ways they make this place our home away from home.
Bless their work and ministry. Bless them.
Let them know they have a place of honor and appreciation in our midst. *Amen.*

You Have Done Marvelously

Lord, you have done marvelous things here at Cord and we thank you:

. . . for teachers who opened doors to knowledge and truth,
. . . for students who emerged as thoughtful and informed,
. . . for dedication and skills and loving labor,
. . . for faithful ministry of our whole community.

Lord, you have done marvelous things here at Cord and we thank you:

. . . for all the students we honor today,
. . . for the knowledge of work well done and recognition earned,
. . . for a place of honor in our midst.

Lord, you have done marvelous things here at Cord and we thank you:

. . . for donor and financial support making scholarships possible,
. . . for parent and family, and prayers and love.

Lord, you have done marvelous things here at Cord and we thank you:

. . . for the difference these students will make in the world,
. . . for using hearts in harmony to be instruments of your peace.

Lord, you have done marvelous things here at Cord and we thank you:

. . . for food that sustains us and sends us forth for loving service,
. . . for love that surrounds us and keeps us on firm foundation.

Lord, you have done marvelous things here at Cord and we thank you!

OFFERTORIES 65

Look at Us Now

Look at our Centennial Campaign volunteers gathered here now.
Look at what we have done:

> We involved 900 volunteers.
> We recruited 17,000 donors.
> We received $58 million in pledges.

Look at what can happen when committed people put hearts in harmony. Look at how people respond when they are *Sent Forth.*

You were the called ones. You were sent forth for a college on the dawn of its centennial. You were sent to tell a story and enlist support. You were called personally and promised personally by an empowering God.

So you went forth with the strategy of Gideon in the Old Testament. You carried your torches. You blew your trumpets. You awakened sleeping supporters with your call to get involved. You made the rallying cry of the centennial echo through the constituency:

> **Sent Forth! Sent Forth! Concordia forever into a new century!**

People responded. Results were gratifying. Look at us now:

> We seized a moment of opportunity to do something for this college we love.
> We gave in a lavishing, cherishing, committed way.
> We enlisted others to do the same.

I hear Jesus saying to us this morning as he accepts our centennial gift, *"You have done a beautiful thing for me!"*

> Well done, faithful ones!
> Just look at us now!
> Look at what we have done!

Be Gracious . . . Not Grumpy

You and I have the power, every time we meet another person, either to be gracious or grumpy. We have the power to edify and build that person up, or to tear down and demolish that person. By what we say and how we say it, and by what we do and how we do it, we can make another feel special and valuable or insignificant and discounted. In this community here, we have a mighty power that we can use positively or negatively in our encounters and work with each person we meet.

As little Christs, what we have to say to people, we need to say graciously, and what we do with people, we need to do graciously. We need to let our words to them and acts to them be a gift . . . respectful, cheerful, uplifting, encouraging, helpful, enriching and appreciative!

I've thought of all the gracious words and acts that our community have done for each other throughout this long winter:

> . . . remember how our community surrounded Tara and Brian's families with gracious words and acts,
>
> . . . remember faculty's gracious words and acts to students,
>
> . . . remember grumpy friend or roommate being responded to with graciousness.

I've thought of all the acts of kindness and graciousness that were done throughout this past year by so many persons and groups, both within our community and out in the community. There have been thousands of acts of graciousness, and help, and random acts of kindness . . . known only to those who were gracious and to those who received their gifts of graciousness.

I'm so aware, personally, these last few days of my ministry here at Concordia, of all the words of graciousness and acts of graciousness I have been receiving. I pray that my ministry has been that way to all of you, somehow, someway, at sometime — gracious and helpful, encouraging and uplifting, kind and understanding.

Remember, every meeting with another person is an opportunity for being gracious rather than grumpy, for helping rather than hurting, for dignifying rather than discounting, for understanding rather than undermining.

The Apostle Paul reminds us to *". . . put on compassion, kindness, gentleness and patience. To all these add love. Let your speech and acts always be gracious."*

I invite us to pray this prayer daily: *Lord, give us tender hearts; let us say and do loving, gracious things that surprise even ourselves. Amen.*

Exodus Thank-Yous

Thank you Lord, for hellos and goodbyes,
for endings and new beginnings,
for all who shared this year with me,
for this last Communion and send-off.

Thank you, Lord, for the supporting love of my family,
for the caring of my friends,
for your presence day by day,
for your forgiveness when I failed.

Thank you, Lord, for sleep when I was tired,
for fun when things got too serious,
for turning my fears into possibilities,
for reassurance when I felt inadequate.

Thank you, Lord, for difficulties that produced dividends,
for pain that produced growth,
for faculty who demanded the best of me,
for successes that encouraged me.

Thank you, Lord, for these Wednesday-evening Communions,
for exciting new adventures and places,
for all the blessings I had this year,
for letting me know that I make a difference.

Thank you, Lord, for being guardian and guide on my journey,
for walking me in new ways into new days,
for giving me the lift and send-off I need,
for doing marvelous things in, through and for me.

Thank you, Lord, Thank You!

A Baccalaureate Surrounding

One more time you come together for a ceremony of endings. With pomp and circumstance, and black-robed vestment and cap, you sit front and center in a position of honor. A host of people surround you.

Look around you, seniors, and see how you are surrounded. Faculty and staff and mentors in your midst. Your whole extended family and friends surround you on all sides. They are a marvelous cheering section, celebrating you and surrounding you with love and presence and hope.

You sit among classmates with whom you have shared your years here. You sit surrounded by those with whom you have laughed and cried, lived and loved, struggled and grown, hoped and dreamed, practiced and played, studied and learned.

Look around you, seniors, and see yourself surrounded. See how God is surrounding you today with a thousand faces and persons. See how God is telling you that as you graduate and leave here, you'll never walk alone. You'll go on your way rejoicing with a thousand prayers following after you.

Yes, you are surrounded. God has touched you and will touch you with a thousand hands in a thousand ways. You will see God's face in a thousand faces. You will see God's face in a thousand faces of nature. You will see God's face in your face. You will hear God's voice whispering in your ear: *"I have called you by name. You are mine. Fear not, I will be with you."*

So let's get up and go. Let's cross over this stage this afternoon, get our diplomas, and journey down the yellow-brick road of life, with brain and heart and courage. Let's journey down the road less traveled with hearts in harmony. Let's walk tall, and live tall, and serve tall in Jesus' name. Let's walk on firm foundation grounded, with love and hope surrounded.

To the Graduates

May God grant you the self-esteem of a cat.

May God give you the perseverance of a nesting swallow.

May your life's song carry like a loon's call.

May your style be that of Pumba.

May your dreams be like those of Simba.

May your talents bloom like spring's first tulips.

May your hope be like spring's first robins.

May your joy be like an Easter worship.

May your lives brighten the world with daring promise.

May God be hidden and compassionate in you.

May God be welcoming and hospitable through you.

May God send you forth to show you what you yet may do.

May God go with you.

May you go with God.

May you go in peace and serve the Lord. Amen.

BENEDICTIONS 73

Go with God

We saw them laugh and celebrate,
And sing and play with talent great.

We felt their stress and overload,
And joblessness and uncertain roads.

We heard refrains of sleepless nights,
And shaky psyches filled with fright.

We heard them cry when loved ones died,
So many during this year's highs.

We were their parents, their best friends,
Who helped their egos heal and mend.

We gave them us instead of things,
So they could trust to use their wings.

We gave them limits, we deepened roots;
We pruned and watered to get fruit.

We gave ourselves, our gifts, our care;
Our presence, our ears were always there.

We made a difference . . . all survived!
And that's good news to feel inside.

And someday one of them will say,
"You made a difference on that day!"

"I'm who I am because you cared;
You sent me forth by how you shared!"

Now go with God; be on your way,
Go forth in peace; serve God each day!

BENEDICTIONS 75

I Promise You

I promise at this altar in the presence of our Lord,
These my special promises! Please listen to my word:

> *I promise that my love will be a window and a door.*
> *I promise that I'll pray for you and celebrate you more.*
>
> *I promise that I'll listen to and understand your word.*
> *I promise you attention so you'll know that you are heard.*
>
> *I promise to be open with and tell you what I need.*
> *I promise to be there for you in thought and word and deed.*
>
> *I promise to be patient and I promise to be cheery.*
> *I promise to be sensitive when you are very weary.*
>
> *I promise to appreciate and thank you more each day.*
> *I promise to reach out and touch and show my love that way.*
>
> *I promise to take time with you to laugh and play and share.*
> *I promise to make plans for ways to show how much I care.*
>
> *I promise you I'll care for me and maintain my good health.*
> *I promise that I'll give to you this special gift of wealth.*
>
> *I promise to commit myself and be your special friend.*
> *I promise that our Lord will be our Savior to the end.*

These promises I give you, you will find each day are true.
They're a promise of my love that says: "I pledge myself to you!"

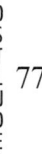

What a Day!

***This is the day that the Lord has made;
Let us rejoice and be glad in it.***
— Psalm 118:24

I awaken and open my eyes.
Sunlight streams through the cabin.
Birds are singing morning matins.

I walk out onto the deck and sit in a choice seat.
The lake is a mirror of deep-blue, crystal-clear water.
The trees stand hushed in morning's quiet.

I am greeted with the gift of a beautiful summer day.
I am witnessing a premier showing never before seen.
The curtains have opened to a new day.

I step into the day as the day the Lord made for me.
I greet the day and accept the day.
I welcome the day with a prayer of awesome thanks:

> *What a day, my Lord, what a day!
> Made for me, O Lord, just this way!*

What a day — as yet untouched and unwritten and unlived, waiting to unfold; to be formed into words!

What a day — waiting to be formulated into plans, energized into activity; waiting to be listened into being, welcomed into participation!

What a day my Lord has made for me in which to rejoice and be glad.

I step into the mystery and surprise of the day with a joyful "yes!"
I begin to unwrap God's gift of today with the eagerness of a child.

I'll make it a good day.
I'll make it a happy day.
I'll make it a "summer postlude" renewing day.

78 SUMMER

God's Glorious Fireworks

Rockets!

Sparklers!

Glow Worms!

Night Parachutes!

Jumping Jacks!

"Get yours for the July 4th weekend!" fireworks ads beckoned.

I didn't need any of them. I had them all, available to me for free . . . at Bad Medicine. There, night after night, God was providing me with an incredible display of fireworks. Let me tell you about God's glorious fireworks.

The night is dark. The stars are twinkling and beaming brightly. The moon hangs like a lantern in the sky, illuminating the woods, sending a shining, shimmering path of light across the lake. I am sitting in my cabin's darkened screened-in porch.

A light flashes briefly, then dies. It shines again, briefly, in another direction, then dies. That flash of light is one tiny firefly.

That firefly is now joined by hundreds of others in a dance of blinking lights. All around me, surrounding me, is a dazzling, twinkling light show. They blink on and off like Christmas tree lights. They are an improvisational theater, a playful dance. They are a fireworks show unparalled in elegance and glory.

They dance for the earth, giving light to its darkness.
They send forth their light, making me part of a community of light.
They are God's glorious fireworks for me this July 4th night.

Fireflies

God blessing us with the gift of a light show,
Like God's word — *"a lamp to our feet and a light to our path,"*
God's goodbyes and God's hellos as they blink on and off:

"Hello . . . God is with you!"
"Goodbye . . . Go with God!"

God promising that we'll never walk alone nor totally in the dark.

We are God's fireflies, God's sparklers, God's fireworks! Each of us is! We can be the light and glowing of God's love shining on others through us. We can let our little lights shine.

80 SUMMER

Ebbing and Flowing

The days of summer pass swiftly. Equilibrium and energy are returning. There is less rushing and more resting. There is time for reflective thought and study. There is an awareness of a healing rhythm of ebb and flow.

    That ebb and flow become so clear during a special vacation. We are on Kaanapli Beach, Maui . . . right by the ocean. Day and night we hear and see the sound of sea and surf ebbing and flowing. The waves crash forward onto the beach and then recede. The waves ebb and flow in constant motion. Rain or shine, evening or morning, high tide or low, the waves rush energetically toward shore. Then they peacefully fall back. There is a constant rhythm: forward . . . backward. Forceful . . . restful.

    This rhythm of ebbing and flowing is mesmerizing and hypnotic. The sound of the sea calms and relaxes us. There is the sense of being healed and renewed by God's creation.

    There is a lesson in that rhythm of ebbing and flowing. That lesson gets forgotten in the hurry and busyness of the school year. Life is like the rhythm of those waves:

> *. . . forward, backward — forceful, restful;*
> *. . . flowing, ebbing — rushing, relaxing;*
> *. . . high tide, low tide — committed, calm;*
> *. . . producing, renewing — powerful, peaceful.*

    When energized, ride the crest of that energy; go with the flow. Get things done, take the initiative, take charge, follow through.

    When drained and depleted and fatigued, fall back with the waves — recede, relax, rest, renew, recharge. Await the next surge of energy, the next onset of a forward rush and flow.

    This is the eternal pattern of God's creation. Job learned that pattern and followed it: "God divides the sea with power."

    The Psalmist experienced it and said: "Be still and know that I am God." In the sea's ebb and flow God shows how to set healing rhythms for our living.

    After rushing, we need to relax. After charging forward, we need to fall back. After working, we need to rest. After we have spent energy in productive activity, we need to retire and recharge. Only then can we be ready for the next surge of energy and flow.

On Eagle's Wings

*As an eagle stirs up its nest and hovers over its young;
as it spreads its wings, takes them up, and bears them
aloft on its pinions, the Lord alone guides . . . .*
— Deuteronomy 32:11

Summer postludes are ending. August preludes are beginning again. There is a change in the air; transitions are everywhere.

A single maple leaf has turned crimson. Dependent baby birds now fly and feed themselves independently. A baby loon no longer rides piggyback on its mother. An eagle's nest, high in a white pine, sits empty.

Soon another school year will begin. Seniors will return in order to get ready to leave. Freshmen will leave home to come to new beginnings. Nests will be emptying and empty, like that of the eagle.

My mind goes back to that eagle's nest. I remember seeing how that nest was constructed. It was built high in that pine with an all-compassing view of the world. The nest was loosely built with branches and sticks and down.

I remember being told about a process of parenting that the eagles used when the eaglets had grown and matured some. The mother eagle leaves the nest, hovers over it, and fans the air around it with her large wings. Her wings create an updraft of wind that stirs the nest and disturbs the eaglets. The stirring wings create currents that dislodge the nest's sticks, which then prick at the eaglet's soft underbellies. Life in the nest becomes uncomfortable enough to make the eaglets leave and fly.

Some of the eaglets refuse to leave, or are afraid to leave the nest. The mother eagle gives these a piggyback ride out of the nest. With the eaglets on her back she glides and soars and then swoops down and away. The young eaglets are left suspended in space where they have no choice but to fly on their own. The mother eagle hovers under them and watches protectively. When an eaglet tires, she piggybacks it back to the safety of the nest. After a bit of rest, the mother eagle repeats the whole process with them again. Soon each one is able to leave the nest and fly on its own.

I think of that scene now as August is nearing. That process is beginning to happen to me, and to other staff. Soon it will happen to senior and freshman.

God is at work like that eagle in life's changes and transitions. God is parenting and pushing out, watching over and surrounding. God is prodding and disrupting, and caring and carrying.

It's time to be nudged into fall's new beginnings.

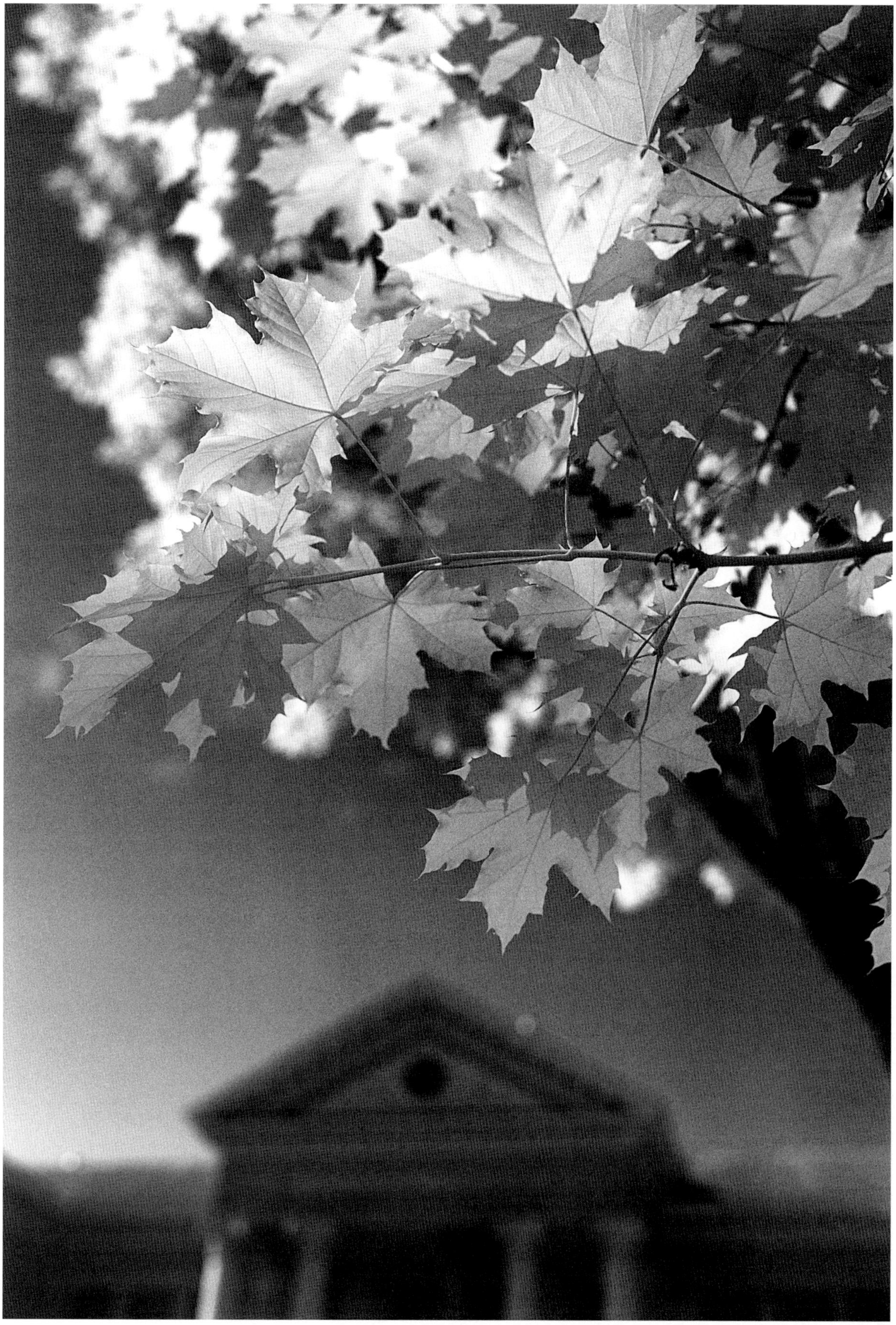

84 SUMMER

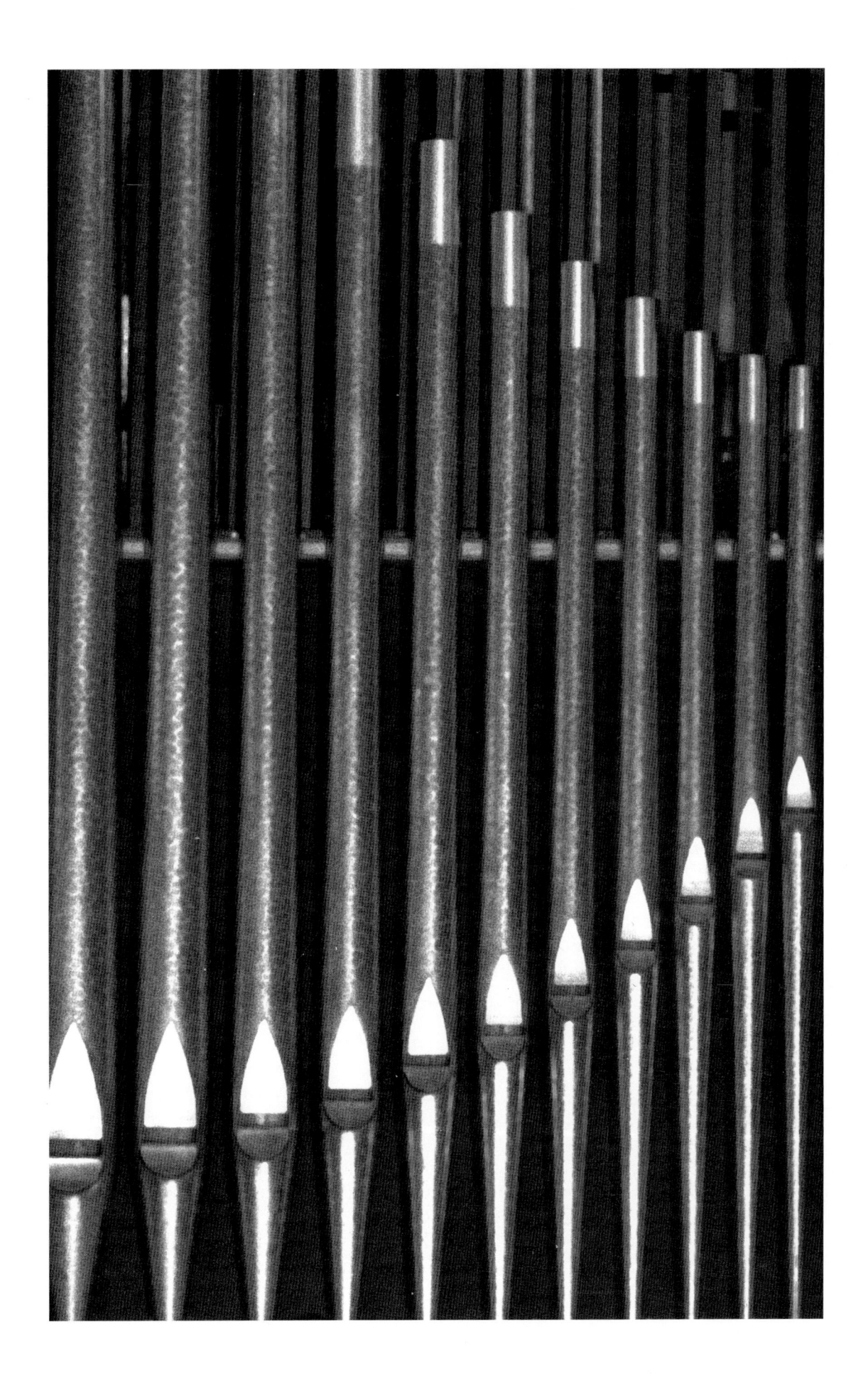

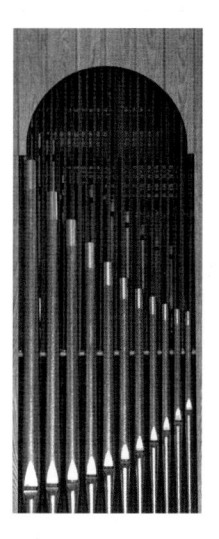

In Retrospect

Throughout my 34 years as pastor and counselor at Concordia, I have listened to students and staff, faculty and alumni tell their stories about how God has called them and spoken to them. These stories come mostly in retrospect. At the time, they weren't even aware that it was God calling them and speaking to them. It was only later that they said they became aware.

It was when they began to look back at situations, and events, and persons, and comments, and interactions, that they began to see how God had been in them — calling and speaking. Most of them said that God's speaking and calling had been so quiet and ordinary, so unspectacular and undramatic, that they did not realize at the time that it had been God speaking and calling.

They talked about Wednesday-night Communions and how meaningful they had been. Yet it was only in retrospect that they began to realize how, through story and song, celebration and quiet, God had been speaking to them and surrounding them.

They talked about times in chapel, or at a lecture, or symposium, or concert, or play, or game. They remembered a word, a phrase, a comment, a melody, a feeling, a question. Now as they think about it in retrospect, it was God in each of these bits and pieces surprising and disrupting, hounding and calling them.

They talked about times when they really felt like happy Cobbers. Again, in retrospect, they saw joy and happiness as the surest sign of God's being with them and speaking to them.

They talked about unexpected interruptions and detours, disappointments and disruptions, changes and transitions that happened to them along the way. Again, in retrospect, they realized how God was there, throughout those times, speaking to them in unexpected and sometimes unwanted and often surprising ways.

I stand at the end of my 34 years of ministry here and also look back in retrospect. I am grateful to God for the privilege of having been God's voice, through my voice, at sometime, to someone, in some situation, in some way.

I pray that my voice has been like that still small voice that has been God calling and speaking to you. I pray that God's voice, through my voice, will continue to go with you.

Amen.

Special Thanks

To *Joe Knutson* for unknowingly starting it,

To *Paul and Mardeth Dovre* for initiating and introducing it,

To *Dave Hetland* for shaping and shepherding it,

To *Doug Fliss* for fine-tuning it,

To *Karen Stensrud* for composing it,

To *Louise Nettleton* for proofing it,

To the *Alumni Office* and *Ernie Mancini* for promoting it,

To *Auxiliary Services, Jane Grant-Shambaugh* and
Linda Widme for marketing it,

To *Dan and Sue Riley, Mike and Mary Lee, Ron and Karen Lee, Walther Prausnitz, Lloyd and Ann Svendsbye, Ralph Hoppe* and *Donald J. Gaetz* for enabling it,

To the *Office of Communciations, Maureen Zimmerman* and
Karla Mickelson for publicizing it,

To the *Photo Lab* and *John Borge* and *Ron Lee* for picturing it,

To *Archives* and *Sharon Hoverson* for researching it,

To *Herb Brokering* and *worship mentors* for inspiring it,

To *Campus Ministry partners* for energizing it,

To *Ann* for living it,

To *Concordia* for sending it forth!

Image Notes and Credits

Each of the photographs featured throughout this volume was selected both for its ability to depict the essence of the meditation it illustrates and for its more literal reference to life on the Concordia campus.

Most of the images came from only a few sources: John Borge (Concordia Photo Lab), Sharon Hoverson (Concordia Archives), Ronald Lee (Pastor Carl's son, who worked in the Concordia Photo Lab while a student and was later employed as a photojournalist) and Karla Mickelson (Concordia Office of Communications).

Front Cover: Carl Lee was called by President Joseph L. Knutson in the spring of 1961 to serve as Concordia's first campus pastor, a position he held until his retirement in 1996. *(John Borge photo)*

Introduction: Dr. Paul J. Dovre was inaugurated as Concordia's eighth president in 1975. *(Borge)*

Preface: Midmorning chapel builds and nourishes the community of faith. *(Hetland Ltd. photo)*

Hosting: With RAs and communicators as hosts, freshman orientation helps new Cobbers make the transition to college life. *(Borge)*

Becoming: Group activities during orientation help strangers become "whobody" friends. *(Concordia Photo Lab)*

Praying: Moving in and saying goodbye to family and friends is part of the college challenge. *(Concordia Photo Lab)*

Serving: Opening Convocation launches each new academic year. *(Borge)*

Beginning: Even the shape of some campus windows encourages focus in daily life. *(Borge)*

This New Day: The morning sun bathes these academic buildings on Concordia's campus. *(Borge)*

An Evening Psalm: Another day ends, darkness comes and the campus pace is slowed. *(Borge)*

A Crystal Gaze: The Crystal Bowl trophy goes to the victor of the annual Moorhead State-Concordia football game. *(Borge)*

Risk Taking a Chance: A blossoming rose reveals its essence and beauty. *(Borge)*

Come! Celebrate the Spirit! Concordia spirit is shown in many ways during homecoming. *(Borge)*

That Special Championship Season: Men's football and women's basketball teams have both won national championships. *(Hetland Ltd. and Borge)*

We Dedicate This Building: Bishop Whipple Hall, Concordia's first building, is re-dedicated following a Centennial Fund remodeling project. *(Borge)*

A Psalm of Relaxation: Body and blood — given freely, accepted gratefully. *(Borge)*

Kyrie! Heal! Wednesday-night Communion provides healing for the campus community. *(Borge)*

Unexpected Interruptions: Unplanned changes to daily schedules can add pressure but may also provide an avenue for new opportunities. *(Borge)*

Thank You: Concordia's campus is aglow with color each autumn. *(Ronald Lee photo)*

Have Mercy: This photo inspired the 1994 Christmas Concert mural based on the theme ***Magnificat: My Soul Proclaims the Greatness of the Lord.*** *(Dr. Susan Vitalis photo)*

Slow Down: Daily life can sometimes be like driving in busy traffic. *(Hetland Ltd.)*

Don't Just Do Something! Stand There! A giant mural visually interprets the themes of Concordia's 69th annual Christmas Concert. *(Hetland Ltd.)*

Come Home with Me for Christmas: Sons Ron, left, and Mike, right, and their families join Ann and Carl at home for Christmas. *(R. Lee)*

Through the Eyes of a Child: Candlelight Communion dramatically symbolizes the birth of the Light of the world. *(Borge and Hetland Ltd.)*

Magi and Graduates . . . Follow a Star: Old Main has come to symbolize Concordia's mission. *(Borge)*

The Magic Slate: Classroom learning is challenging, exciting and filled with possibilities. *(Borge)*

Blessed Are You: Under a blanket of snow, Fjelstad Hall seems a symbol of peace. *(R. Lee)*

Magi Journey Eastward: Emblazoned upon a Russian Language Village flag is a golden star. *(Borge)*

In Loving Memory: *Haus Katja* was constructed as a memorial to Kathy Rutherford by staff and students at the German Language Village, where she had served as a counselor. *(Hetland Ltd.)*

Come, Lord Jesus: A May Seminar visit to a cathedral becomes a spiritual experience. *(Borge)*

Are You Listening? Although each piano key is discrete, if in tune the keys can together provide magnificent music. *(Hetland Ltd.)*

I Wonder About . . . Concordia's many students often volunteer their time and talents at local nursing homes and hospitals. *(Borge)*

Be My Valentine: We need to share a daily valentine moment. *(Hetland Ltd.)*

Mountaintops and Valleys: Mountaintop experiences can prepare us for living in the valley. *(R. Lee)*

Living Bible Verses: Many Cobbers spend midsemester breaks traveling to remote parts of the country to work on Habitat for Humanity projects. *(Kris Pond-Burtis photo)*

Good Guilt: Clown faces at Church Youth Days can mask true feelings. *(Concordia Photo Lab)*

Encouraging Words: Christ performs a healing in this scene from Cyrus Running's mural in the Ivers Science Building. *(Hetland Ltd.)*

Special Crosses: We lift high the cross in sacrament and service. *(Hetland Ltd.)*

Mommy! Daddy! This towering stained-glass window depicting the Holy Trinity was designed by David Hetland, a Concordia alum. It is located in the Christian Life Center of Moorhead's Trinity Lutheran Church, the church home of many Cobbers. *(Hetland Ltd.)*

An Aloha Easter Experience: Palm fronds symbolize the beginning of Holy Week. Palm trees provide a Good Friday background for an Easter sunrise service on Wailea Beach, Maui. *(photos by R. Lee and Pastor Carl Lee)*

A Prayer for Spring: Frozen bicycles await spring thaw on Concordia's campus. *(R. Lee photo)*

You Have Done Marvelously: Positioned in the center of campus and topped by a cross, Concordia's Campanile proclaims the lordship of Christ here. The college's signature does likewise. *(Borge)*

Look At Us Now: Volunteers celebrate the successful conclusion of the Centennial Fund. *(Borge)*

A Baccalaureate Surrounding: Seniors are surrounded by faculty, families and friends at the baccalaureate service. *(Borge)*

A Senior's Send-off: Graduates share one last embrace before being "sent forth." *(Borge)*

To the Graduates: President Dovre presents diplomas and offers congratulations. *(Borge)*

Go With God: This Christmas Concert program echoes the closing blessing used at all campus worship services. *(Hetland Ltd.)*

I Promise You: Carl Lee and Ann Teigen exchanged marriage vows August 16, 1953.

What a Day! A new day is reflected in still water. *(R. Lee)*

God's Glorious Fireworks: Homecoming fireworks brighten the campus sky. *(Erin Conroy photo)*

Ebbing and Flowing: An ocean's tide suggests the rhythm of daily life. *(R. Lee)*

On Eagle's Wings: Turning leaves signal transition to a new season — in nature and in lives. *(Borge)*

In Retrospect: Centrum organ pipes sound the call to worship as we live. *(Borge)*

Back Cover: Backyard barbecues were a regular part of life for the Lee family: Mike (with Mouse), Ron, Pastor Carl and Ann. *(Concordia Archives photo)*